really easy play in no trumps

Really Easy Play in No Trumps is for everybody who wants to improve their card play, from complete beginners to those who realise they need a firmer grasp of how to play the cards.

Starting from the very first principles, Really Easy Play in No Trumps explains how to plan the play of a bridge hand in no trumps. Every point is illustrated by example hands to show how these principles work out in practice.

Each hand includes the bidding using simple modern Acol, the English Bridge Union's recommended starting point for those learning the game.

The book ends with 24 practice hands that you can make up and play with friends and then study to see what you should have done.

Enjoy the book, then go out and enjoy playing bridge.

John Pain
EBU Teachers' Association Manager

Sandra Landy
Series Editor

Really Easy Play in No Trumps

First Published by the English Bridge Union in England in 1999.

© English Bridge Union Ltd 1999, second edition 2002

ISBN 0-9543685-0-9

Designed by Milestone Strategic Creative Design of Beaconsfield.

Typeset by Wakewing of High Wycombe.

Printed and bound by Buckingham Colour Group Ltd.

Other books in the Really Easy Bridge Series

Really Easy Bidding 1998, second edition 1999,
    reprinted 2001
Really Easy Practice 1 1999
Really Easy Mistakes 2000
Really Easy Practice 2 2000
Really Easy Modern Acol 2001
Really Easy Play with Trumps 2001
Really Easy Defence 2002

The English Bridge Union
Broadfields,
Bicester Road
Aylesbury HP19 8AZ
Tel: 01296 317217
Email: bfa@ebu.co.uk

Really Easy
Play in
No Trumps

contents

1 how to use this book

Bridge, the most rewarding of all card games, has two parts. The first is the bidding (the 'auction') which will end with someone declaring a contract, which he or she will then try to make when the hand is played.

This book is about making tricks (the play) and not about how you came to contract to make them. None the less, with most of the examples, the auction is given based on simple modern Acol.

This book is exclusively about playing in no trump contracts, since this is a good basis on which to develop a sound understanding of how tricks are won and lost. Our follow up book Really Easy Play with Trumps looks at the special techniques needed when there is a trump suit.

hand diagrams for planning the play

Sometimes all four hands are shown, but frequently, only the East-West hands are given since they are, together with the bidding and the opening lead, the only data available when the play of the hand is planned.

For example:

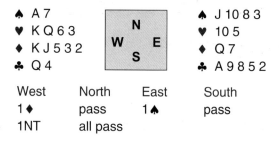

♠ A 7			♠ J 10 8 3
♥ K Q 6 3			♥ 10 5
♦ K J 5 3 2			♦ Q 7
♣ Q 4			♣ A 9 8 5 2

West	North	East	South
1♦	pass	1♠	pass
1NT	all pass		

North leads ♦3.

In all the hand diagrams in this book West is always the dealer and always becomes the declarer. When presented with a problem, you are assumed to be sitting in that position.

how to use this book

- Always have a pack of cards by you as you read – lay out the hands to follow the play more clearly
- Bridge is a partnership game – read this book with your partner and enjoy learning together
- Play bridge – practice makes perfect.

2 counting top winners

What are 'top winners'? They are the cards which, after the dummy hand is exposed, the declarer can see are certain to take tricks.

A K 3 2	Q J 5 4

In a no trump contract, this suit has four top winners. Play the ace and king and then the queen and jack. Or, it matters not, play the queen and jack and then the ace and king.

On the other hand,

K Q 3 2	J 10 5 4

has no top winners until the opponent's ace has been played.

For the moment, we are concerned only with cards that start as certain winners and not those that may become winners.

Let's start with an example:

```
    ♠ A Q              ♠ K J
    ♥ K 8 6 4    N     ♥ A 7 3
    ♦ 6 5 3    W   E   ♦ A K 4 2
    ♣ A 7 3 2    S     ♣ 9 8 6 5
```

West	North	East	South
1NT	pass	3NT	all pass

North leads ♠5.

The bidding is correct. There are more points in the combined hands than are needed to bid to game since 25 points is often enough and East-West have 28. But the contract will not be made. The two hands include the four top cards in spades, the two top cards in both hearts and diamonds and the top card in clubs. That totals nine and equals the number of tricks required but, unfortunately, nine top cards does not equate to nine top winners (the sure tricks that can be taken without losing the lead). The problem lies in the spade suit which, despite its ten points and its four top cards, can produce only two tricks. Both hands have just two cards so a top card must be played on a top card whenever spades are played.

Therefore, although there are nine top cards between the two hands, there are only seven top winners available. An extra trick might develop during the play, but certainly not two.

Let's amend the two hands slightly. Count the points and you will find that they are exactly the same as in our first ill-fated example; the distribution has changed but not the point count.

♠ A Q		♠ K J 2
♥ K 8 6 4		♥ A 7 3
♦ 6 5 3		♦ A K 4
♣ A 7 3 2		♣ 9 8 6 5

Here, all we have done is made the two of diamonds (♦2) into the two of spades (♠2). Now, however, the spade suit is good for three tricks. Only one top card falls on another.

Still with the same number of points, see the effect of giving East another small spade.

♠ A Q		♠ K J 3 2
♥ K 8 6 4	N	♥ A 7
♦ 6 5 3	W E	♦ A K 4
♣ A 7 3 2	S	♣ 9 8 6 5

Now spades will produce four tricks. The combined hands have the nine top winners necessary to make 3NT, four in spades, two in both hearts and diamonds and one in clubs.

You cannot take more tricks in a suit than the number of cards in the longest holding.

quiz

How many top tricks are there in the hands below?

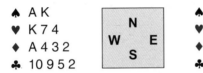

	♠ A K		♠ Q J
	♥ K 7 4	N	♥ Q J 10
	♦ A 4 3 2	W E	♦ K 7 6 5
	♣ 10 9 5 2	S	♣ A K Q J

Despite the four top honours there are only two top tricks in spades, since there are only two spades in each hand. There are no top hearts. Two top diamonds and four top clubs make a total of eight top tricks on this deal.

	♠ A K		♠ Q J 5 4
	♥ K 7 4	N	♥ Q J
	♦ A 4 3 2	W E	♦ K 7 6
	♣ 10 9 5 2	S	♣ A K Q J

Now that East has four spades there are four top winners in spades instead of two and that makes a total of ten top tricks.

	♠ A K		♠ Q J 10
	♥ A K	N	♥ Q J 10 9
	♦ A K Q 6	W E	♦ 5 4 3 2
	♣ J 10 9 8 7	S	♣ 6 5

Two top spades, two top hearts, three top diamonds and no top clubs makes seven top tricks. If you counted three in spades and four in hearts you are wrong. Since there is no entry to the East hand to cash those top tricks, we cannot count them. Top tricks only count if we can reach them to cash them.

♠ A K
♥ A K 6
♦ A K Q
♣ J 10 9 8 7

♠ Q J 10
♥ Q J 10 9
♦ 5 4 3 2
♣ 6 5

Look what a difference it makes if the red six is in hearts. Now there are three top spades, four top hearts, three top diamonds and no clubs. That ♥6 provides the entry to reach both the spade and heart winners.

♠ K Q 7 2
♥ K Q 3
♦ K 2
♣ Q J 10 9

♠ J 10 9 8
♥ J 10 9 8
♦ Q J 10 9 8
♣ –

No top winners! But that doesn't mean you cannot win any tricks. There are plenty of tricks available here once the missing aces have been driven out.

3 cashing top winners

Look at this hand:

	West		East
♠	6 5 3		♠ A 4
♥	K 8 6 4	N	♥ A 7
♦	A Q	W E	♦ K J 10 3 2
♣	A 7 3 2	S	♣ J 8 6 5

West	North	East	South
1NT	pass	3NT	all pass

North leads ♠Q.

West counts the sure tricks. There is one top winner in spades (♠A), two in hearts (♥A and ♥K) and one in clubs (♣A). There are another five top winners in diamonds (A, K, Q, J and 10), which can all be won since East has five cards in the suit. With a satisfactory count of nine sure tricks, declarer has simply to make sure of taking them in the right order.

East's ♠A is therefore played followed by ♦2, won by West's ♦A. ♦Q is cashed and East's hand is entered with ♥A to cash ♦K J 10 that are all winners.

Note how declarer should play the diamond suit by cashing the two top winners in the West hand first. With ♦K in East, ♦A and ♦Q become of equal rank: ♦Q could equally have won the second trick. This may seem obvious but many players new to the game tend to cash top winners according to their seniority: an ace before a king in the same suit. This can cause problems:

A Q J 10 2   K 3

This suit is certain to supply five tricks, but if West plays the ace and then the two, the suit has been blocked. West will have three top winners in his hand (Q J 10) but has to have some means of getting to them. West should play the two to East's king and then the three to the ace to take the four top winners in his hand.

K Q 3 2	A J 4

Start with the ace and then the jack.

When you have top winners in a suit in both hands, take the top winner(s) in the hand with the shorter suit first.

In the example on the previous page, after cashing the ace and queen of diamonds, West needed the lead to be in dummy (East's hand); an entry was required to win the other three diamonds. Let's amend the hands slightly:

	♠ K 5 3			♠ A 4
	♥ A 8 6 4	**N**		♥ J 7
	♦ A Q	**W E**		♦ K J 10 3 2
	♣ A 7 3 2	**S**		♣ 9 8 6 5

West	North	East	South
1♥	pass	2♦	pass
3NT	all pass		

North leads ♠Q.

Does it matter whether declarer wins the trick with East's ♠A or West's ♠K?

The same nine tricks are available but to be certain of making them, declarer needs to keep East's ♠A as an entry to dummy. He needs that entry to take three more diamonds once ♦A and ♦Q have been won. You must make a plan before playing to the first trick, and then call for ♠4 to be played from dummy.

Try this hand:

	North		
♠ A 7		N	♠ 5 4 3 2
♥ A Q 3 2	W	E	♥ K 7
♦ A K 3 2		S	♦ Q J
♣ 9 8 7			♣ A 6 5 4 3

West	North	East	South
1♥	pass	1♠	pass
2NT	pass	3NT	all pass

North leads ♠K.

There are nine top tricks and all you have to do is take them. However, there are communication problems. Anyone minded to play ♥A, after winning ♠A, will arrive at a dead end. Try it! You have to develop one spade trick, three heart tricks, four diamond tricks and one club trick.

Win ♠A, take ♦Q and ♦J, cash ♥K and enter West's hand with the second heart. Nine certain tricks are there provided care is taken in the order in which they are won.

Here's an exciting hand.

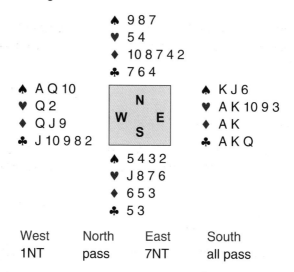

```
                    ♠ 9 8 7
                    ♥ 5 4
                    ♦ 10 8 7 4 2
                    ♣ 7 6 4
  ♠ A Q 10                           ♠ K J 6
  ♥ Q 2            N                 ♥ A K 10 9 3
  ♦ Q J 9        W   E               ♦ A K
  ♣ J 10 9 8 2       S               ♣ A K Q
                    ♠ 5 4 3 2
                    ♥ J 8 7 6
                    ♦ 6 5 3
                    ♣ 5 3
```

West	North	East	South
1NT	pass	7NT	all pass

North leads ♠9.

When East tabled his hand, West saw riches beyond his wildest dreams. A count gave fourteen top winners when only thirteen were required and West began to take them: first spades then hearts (correctly starting with ♥Q) then … ouch!

South won the last two tricks with ♥J and ♠5.

'Better luck next time,' said East.

Now … there's a partner whom West will cherish. Can you do better? Put the cards out and try before reading on.

Just make sure you cash the tricks in a sensible order. For example:

Win with ♠Q. Take ♥Q and play ♥2 to ♥A. Then play ♥K. You have been counting hearts so you know someone still has ♥J. Now play ♦A and ♦K, ♣A, ♣K and ♣Q, and ♠K. Cross to hand with ♠J to ♠A and take the remaining club and diamond tricks.

Congratulations rather than consolations from partner!

quiz

How many top winners do you have in the suit shown? In what order must the tricks be cashed to be certain of making all the top winners?

♠ Q 2   ♠ A K J 10 3

There are five top winners.

Cash ♠Q first and then play ♠2 to enter the East hand and cash ♠A K J 10 to make all five tricks however the spades break.

♠ K 2   ♠ A Q J 4

There are four top winners.

Cash ♠K first then ♠2 to enter the East hand and cash ♠A K J.

♠ A Q 4   ♠ K J 10 3 2

There are five top winners.

Cash ♠A then ♠Q then play ♠4 to make East's three remaining winners.

♠ A K 6 4   ♠ Q J 10

There are four top winners provided you play ♠Q first, then ♠J and finally ♠10 overtaking it with ♠K to cash ♠A.

♠ A Q   ♠ K J 10 3 2

It looks like there are five top winners but they are not 100% certain if there is no other suit with which you can get to the East hand. Cash ♠A and then play ♠Q, putting ♠K on ♠Q to gain an entry. Because you have to overtake the queen you will not make five tricks if one opponent has five or six spades.

4 establishing extra top winners

Most of the time, the number of top tricks is fewer than the number of tricks needed to make your contract. You have to look for opportunities to make extra tricks.

High cards, which do not start life as top winners, can be established to become winners.

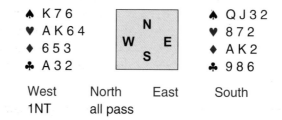

♠ K 7 6		♠ Q J 3 2
♥ A K 6 4	N	♥ 8 7 2
♦ 6 5 3	W E	♦ A K 2
♣ A 3 2	S	♣ 9 8 6

West	North	East	South
1NT	all pass		

North leads ♦Q.

It is a modest contract and dummy makes a reassuring sight.

Do not cash your sure tricks and hope that all will come right in the end.

Count your certain tricks: they come to five. Two more are needed and the spade suit can provide them. If you can make a defender win ♠A, by playing any of the king, queen or jack (which, for this purpose are of equal rank), the two remaining high cards in the suit are established as winners. Having identified both the problem and the source of the extra tricks, you must set about the task of establishing those extra tricks immediately.

Therefore, you win the first trick with ♦K and, straight away, play a small spade to your ♠K. If North wins ♠A, you win whatever is the next card played and happily cash ♠Q and ♠J and your other top winners. If ♠K wins the second trick, play another spade towards ♠Q J 3 in dummy, intending to play the queen or jack if North follows with a small card. The fact that a defender, with ♠A, may choose to let you win both of the first two spades is a matter of no concern. Having made the two extra tricks required, you abandon the suit and take your other top winners.

What has happened here is that, having made your count of available tricks, you are prepared to lose the lead deliberately to set up extra tricks. This is not a decision that comes easily. It is similar to the fear of flying: you worry that you have no control over subsequent events. It is true that there are occasions, and we will look at them in due course, when this fear has some justification. Here, however, you can see that the lead can be lost in perfect safety. You are bound to win it back because you hold the top winners in all the other suits.

We said, with the example hand, that after winning the first trick you must play the spade suit immediately. You would be sailing perilously close to the rocks if you decided to postpone it awhile, maybe by cashing a top winner or two to get the feel of things. For sure, you would be establishing top tricks; but, this time, for the defenders!

When you need to establish an extra winner(s), you must do so before cashing your certain top winners in the other suits.

The mistake of taking certain tricks before establishing others is made so often by beginners that it is worth another example.

What we will do is simply to remove the top winners from the East-West hands and see what might be left, and the probable outcome. This might be the complete deal:

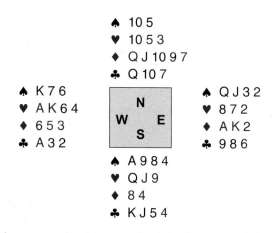

Declarer is assumed to have cashed the five sure tricks (marked in red) before turning his attention to setting up the two spade winners that should have been established at the start. This is the position after everybody has played five cards:

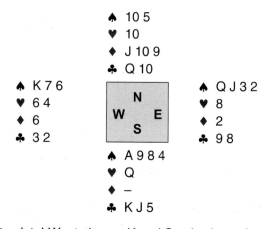

It is now too late! West plays ♠K and South wins ♠A, cashes ♥Q (which has become a top winner) and then leads ♣5. North wins this trick and three more diamonds, on which South discards three spades, and then leads ♣Q. South overtakes this with the ♣K and wins the last trick with the ♣J. Declarer ends up with five tricks and the defence with eight.

- Count your sure winners.

- If the answer is fewer than you need, ask yourself whether extra winners can be established.

- If they can, play to set them up before taking your certain tricks.

- Check that there is no problem in regaining the lead.

Certainly, there are hands when there is no hope of making enough tricks and you take whatever is available. There are hands where all is lost if you lose the lead. Both are rare. They also assume that you have thought about, and recognised, the problem at the outset. You have counted and considered, but rejected, the possibility of establishing extra tricks.

The pulse rate goes up when a slam has been bid:

```
       ♠ K 2              ┌─────────┐       ♠ Q 4 3
       ♥ A K Q 4          │    N    │       ♥ J 7 3
       ♦ Q J 10        W  │       E │       ♦ A K 2
       ♣ A J 7 6          │    S    │       ♣ K Q 3 2
                          └─────────┘

       West       North      East       South
       2NT        pass       6NT        all pass
```

North leads ♥10.

West can count eleven top winners and the vital twelfth can be established by playing one top spade. West does this before taking the sure tricks in the other three suits.

Let's make things a little tougher. Sometimes two of the defenders' top winners in a suit need to be driven out.

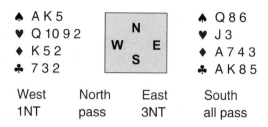

	♠ A K 5			♠ Q 8 6
	♥ Q 10 9 2			♥ J 3
	♦ K 5 2			♦ A 7 4 3
	♣ 7 3 2			♣ A K 8 5

West	North	East	South
1NT	pass	3NT	all pass

North leads ♠J.

On this hand a count of the sure winners comes to seven but two more can be established in hearts. The combined holding lacks the two top winners but contains the next four highest cards. If both the ace and the king can be driven out, by using two of those cards, the remaining two will provide the extra winners required.

This will mean giving up the lead twice but West can see that there is no danger because, after the opening lead, the two top winners in all the three other suits are held.

Therefore, declarer wins the opening lead with East's ♠Q and, following the advice given previously (start with the top card(s) from the shorter suit), immediately leads ♥J. This should result in a defender winning with ♥A or ♥K and it doesn't matter which card next appears on the table; West wins and plays another top heart.

If the defence holds off winning ♥A or ♥K or both, West abandons the suit once two tricks in it have been safely secured.

What about this hand?

	♠ A K 5			♠ Q 8 6
	♥ Q 10 9 2			♥ K J 3
	♦ K 10 2			♦ Q 9 3
	♣ 9 7 3			♣ A K 10 5

In the same 3NT contract and after the same ♠J lead, the tally of top winners is a miserable five. You need four extra tricks and the plan will be to set up three tricks in hearts, by driving out the ace, and one trick in diamonds with the same technique. You should start with your stronger suit first and when you can see three heart tricks in the bag, you establish the one trick needed in diamonds.

You will, of course, attend to these matters before, voluntarily, playing your sure winners in clubs and spades!

If you remain unconvinced, make up some possible North-South hands. You will discover that, whatever cards you give them, West, after an initial spade lead and playing sensibly, cannot fail to make 3NT.

It is not necessarily aces and kings that need to be driven out.

♠ A K 5		♠ Q 7 6 2
♥ J 10 9 2	N	♥ A 3
♦ K 10 2	W E	♦ Q J 3
♣ 9 7 3	S	♣ A K 10 5

West	North	East	South
pass	pass	1♠	pass
2NT	pass	3NT	all pass

North leads ♠J.

There is some work to be done to make this contract. The tally of top winners is only six. West can establish two more tricks by driving out ♦A, but needs one further trick.

Look to the heart suit to provide it. Declarer can afford to lose to both ♥K and ♥Q in the interests of making one certain trick with ♥A and another from that ♥J 10 9 combination.

West wins the opening lead and plays ♥2 to ♥A and leads another heart. It will lose to ♥K or ♥Q but, as soon as the lead is regained, West plays another heart to drive out the opposition's second winning card in the suit. Subsequently, West plays diamonds to establish two tricks in that suit.

It is better to start to establish the suit in which you have to lose two tricks (hearts) rather than that in which you need only lose one trick (diamonds). Establishing a diamond trick first would give the defenders time, since you have to lose the lead twice more, to establish their own winners in diamonds.

You might even find yourself completely bereft of top winners.

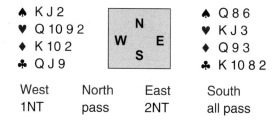

	♠ K J 2		♠ Q 8 6
	♥ Q 10 9 2	N	♥ K J 3
	♦ K 10 2	W E	♦ Q 9 3
	♣ Q J 9	S	♣ K 10 8 2

West	North	East	South
1NT	pass	2NT	all pass

North leads ♠3.

Here, you have to try to establish tricks in all four suits. Every time you gain the lead, you must drive out an enemy ace. You should start with your stronger suits, hearts or clubs, which can produce the most tricks.

Say that you play hearts immediately you get the lead. As soon as ♥A is played, and you recover the lead, leave hearts alone for the present and play on clubs to drive out ♣A.

Suppose the full hand was:

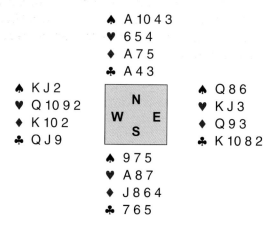

```
                    ♠ A 10 4 3
                    ♥ 6 5 4
                    ♦ A 7 5
                    ♣ A 4 3
    ♠ K J 2                         ♠ Q 8 6
    ♥ Q 10 9 2       N              ♥ K J 3
    ♦ K 10 2      W     E           ♦ Q 9 3
    ♣ Q J 9          S              ♣ K 10 8 2
                    ♠ 9 7 5
                    ♥ A 8 7
                    ♦ J 8 6 4
                    ♣ 7 6 5
```

The ♠3 lead goes to ♠6 from dummy, ♠9 from South and you win ♠J. You play ♥2 to dummy's ♥K and South will probably win and return ♠7 (North's suit). North will win ♠A and lead another spade. You win ♠K and now start to establish some club winners by playing ♣Q. North will take ♣A and has ♠10 to cash.

On this trick you have to make a discard from both hands but your objectives have been completed. This is probably the position:

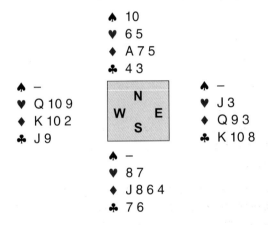

```
                    ♠ 10
                    ♥ 6 5
                    ♦ A 7 5
                    ♣ 4 3
  ♠ —                              ♠ —
  ♥ Q 10 9         N               ♥ J 3
  ♦ K 10 2     W       E           ♦ Q 9 3
  ♣ J 9            S               ♣ K 10 8
                    ♠ —
                    ♥ 8 7
                    ♦ J 8 6 4
                    ♣ 7 6
```

North is about to play ♠10.

You have won two spade tricks and your hearts and clubs are now winners. It is perfectly safe to discard a diamond from both hands and the best that North can do is to cash the remaining ace for the fifth defensive trick.

5 small cards can take tricks

In a no trump contract, even the insignificant two is a certain trick, if it is the only remaining card in a suit.

A K Q J 2	6 5 4 3

There are thirteen cards in a suit. Here, East-West have nine of them, so North-South have four between them. When West plays the four top winners, there are no cards left in the North-South hands, however the suit divides. Therefore the two is a certain fifth trick to go with the four top winners. When you look at such a suit, in planning the play, you count it for five certain tricks.

Remove a card from East's hand:

A K Q J 2	5 4 3

Now, with East-West having only eight cards in the suit, there is a slight possibility that either North or South holds all five of the remaining cards. You will, rightly, think that this is highly unlikely and again, when you plan, you can assume that the two will become a winner and that the suit will produce five tricks.

In fact only four times in a hundred will the suit break so badly that you don't have five tricks.

As we decrease the total number of cards held in the two hands, the odds that the small cards will become winners (because nobody can follow suit) must get smaller.

A K Q J 2	4 3

You should still expect that, after West has played four top winners, the two would be an extra trick. With six cards in the combined North-South hands, they will need to divide 6-0 or 5-1 to prevent this. Again, you would count this suit to be good for five tricks.

The bad breaks stopping you from making five tricks will happen fewer than one time in five.

Remove another card from the East hand:

A K Q J 2	3

That two is becoming less certain to win a trick, but the odds are still good. There are seven cards in the North-South hands, but they are more likely to be divided 4-3 than any other combination, but the odds of making five tricks have reduced to six times in ten.

Finally we come to:

A K Q J 2	Void

There are eight cards in this suit held by North-South but now the odds that the two will become a winner are not good. It is much more likely that the North-South cards will divide 5-3 or worse, than that they will split 4-4. When planning the play, you might hope to make five tricks from this suit but you should not rely on this as it only happens about one third of the time.

You can see that a long suit can be as good as having a top winner. We had this example earlier:

The spade suit will provide four tricks. But, suppose we remove one top winner (♦K), from the East hand, but give it an extra spade. Now we have:

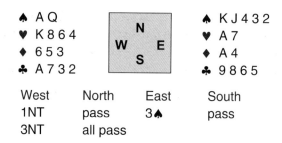

♠ A Q
♥ K 8 6 4
♦ 6 5 3
♣ A 7 3 2

♠ K J 4 3 2
♥ A 7
♦ A 4
♣ 9 8 6 5

West	North	East	South
1NT	pass	3♠	pass
3NT	all pass		

North leads ♦ Q.

Although there are now three fewer combined points, there are nine probable tricks. You know that small cards can become winners and that, with this combined spade holding, one defender will have to hold at least five spades to prevent you making five tricks in the suit. If West plays ♠A and ♠Q, and both defenders follow suit, nine tricks are assured since a 5-1 split has been eliminated and the spades must now be dividing 3-3 or 4-2.

The full deal shows how the play should go:

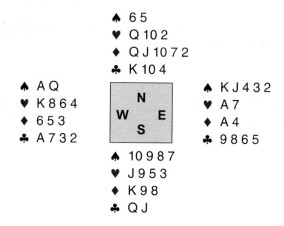

♠ 6 5
♥ Q 10 2
♦ Q J 10 7 2
♣ K 10 4

♠ A Q
♥ K 8 6 4
♦ 6 5 3
♣ A 7 3 2

♠ K J 4 3 2
♥ A 7
♦ A 4
♣ 9 8 6 5

♠ 10 9 8 7
♥ J 9 5 3
♦ K 9 8
♣ Q J

West counts the sure tricks. There are four in hearts, diamonds and clubs and the expectation is that the distribution in spades will allow that suit to produce five more. East's ♦A is therefore played followed by ♠2, won by West's ♠A. ♠Q is cashed and West, noting that both opponents have followed suit, plays ♥4, winning with dummy's ace, to cash ♠K, ♠J and ♠4, discarding small cards from hand. Seven tricks have been won and ♥K and ♣A are still to follow.

quiz

How likely is it that the following suit holdings will yield five tricks?

♣ A J 10 3 2   ♣ K Q 4

You are certain to make five tricks by playing K Q first then the A J 10.

♣ A J 4 3 2   ♣ K Q 5

Only if one opponent holds ♣ 10 9 8 7 6 will you fail to make five tricks. 19 times out of 20 you will succeed.

♣ A 5 4 3 2   ♣ K Q 6

You will make five tricks when the five missing clubs break 3-2 – about six times in ten.

♣ A Q J 9   ♣ K 10 8

Despite having all the high cards you can never make more than four tricks in no trumps.

6 establishing small cards as winners

Since small cards can take tricks, any suit in which you have more cards than the defenders is an opportunity to set up extra tricks. You must be prepared to lose a trick in a suit (and be content to lose the lead in so doing) in the interest of making extra tricks. There are some particular suit combinations that will arise regularly in a no trump contract. Here's an example:

A K Q 3 2	6 5 4

When, in the planning stage, you count your likely tricks, you would expect to make five tricks in the suit more often than not. If the defenders' five cards in the suit divide 3-2, both of West's small cards will be winners after ace, king and queen have been played.

However, you may need this suit to produce only four tricks and the chances for this are very good indeed. What you do is to play two of West's top winners and, if both opponents follow, you happily play the third knowing that the three and two have become tricks. But, if one defender fails to follow suit to the second top winner, the suit has divided 4-1. This means that you must lose one trick but you can still make four tricks. You play off West's third top winner and then a small card. This loses but the second small card is a winner. What you have done, by deliberately losing a trick, is to establish a small card as a winner. This is the same technique as establishing winners by driving out the opponents' high cards.

What if one defender discarded on West's first top winner? You have run into a very unlucky break and have to resign yourself to the fact that the only tricks will be A K Q. As we saw in the last chapter, this only happens one time in twenty-five.

Plan the play with these hands:

♠ Q 9 2			♠ A K 6
♥ J 10 3	N		♥ Q 9 8 5
♦ A K Q 5 4	W E		♦ 6 3 2
♣ A K	S		♣ 8 7 6

West	North	East	South
1♦	pass	1♥	pass
3NT	all pass		

North leads ♣Q.

There are eight top winners and you calculate that ♦5 and ♦4 are very likely to become extra winners. After winning the first trick, West plays ♦A and ♦K, but North fails to follow suit on the second round. This is not a disaster since only one extra trick from the diamond suit will suffice. So, West continues with ♦Q and then ♦4. South will win this trick but, when declarer regains the lead, ♦5 is established as a winner and the ninth trick.

Note that you must start playing diamonds at trick two. While the odds are good that you will make all five tricks in the suit, it is not a certainty. You must test this suit first while you know that you can regain the lead if a diamond trick must be lost.

Let's look at the possible tricks available from other combined long suits.

A K Q 5 2	4 3

It is against the odds that this combined 7-card suit will produce five tricks. The defenders' cards would need to be divided 3-3 to enable the five and two to become winners.

However, if you can afford to lose one trick in this suit, the odds of making a total of four tricks are good. More than four times out of five (84%) you will make your contract.

Knowing the odds on how the suit will split, we can look at three different situations.

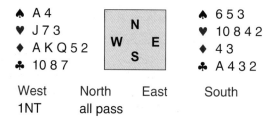

♠ A 4		♠ 6 5 3
♥ J 7 3		♥ 10 8 4 2
♦ A K Q 5 2		♦ 4 3
♣ 10 8 7		♣ A 4 3 2

West	North	East	South
1NT	all pass		

North leads ♠Q. South plays ♠9 on first trick.

With only five top winners, you have to hope that both the two small diamonds will become winners. This means that you should cash the three top diamonds and pray for a 3-3 break. This is against the odds, but the only chance.

♠ 7 4 2		♠ A 5 3
♥ J 7		♥ A 8 4 2
♦ A K Q 5 2		♦ 4 3
♣ A 10 8		♣ 7 4 3 2

Same bidding. North leads ♠Q. South plays ♠9 on the first trick.

You have six top winners and, therefore, only one of West's small diamonds needs to provide an extra trick. You can, again, play the three top diamond winners. If they happen to break 3-3, a total of eight tricks will result. If they divide, as expected 4-2, you simply play a fourth, small diamond and the fifth diamond is established as a winner. Losing the lead is not a problem. The defenders will take some spade tricks, but not enough to defeat you. You hold the aces in hearts and clubs to regain the lead.

```
♠ A 7 4              ♠ 6 5 3
♥ J 7        N       ♥ A 8 4 2
♦ A K Q 5 2  W   E   ♦ 4 3
♣ 10 8 7        S    ♣ A 4 3 2
```

West is in the same 1NT contract with the same ♠Q lead.

This requires a different technique. Can you see why?

Again, the diamond suit needs to produce only one extra trick and, again, you can afford to lose one diamond in the interests of making four. Now, however, you should give up the trick that you are prepared to lose by playing a small diamond from both hands as soon as you get the lead. There are two reasons for this. Firstly, the odds are that the diamonds will divide 4-2 rather than 3-3. Secondly, if they do divide 4-2, and you have to lose one trick to set up the extra one, you have to get to West's hand to take it.

The only certain entry to the West hand vanishes after you are forced to win ♠A. Therefore, you must play a small diamond from both hands so that the diamond suit itself provides the vital entry back to the West hand and its diamond winners.

Your decision how to play these three hands rests simply on the number of tricks that you need from the key suit. On the first hand, you cannot afford to lose a trick and therefore you must play against the odds. On the second hand, you can try for an extra trick without risk. On the third hand, when you have an entry problem, it would be foolish not to play for the more likely distribution.

With a combined holding of seven cards in a suit, the opponents' cards are much more likely to divide 4-2 than 3-3.

making small cards winners

Armed with probabilities of how long suits will divide, you can plan from the start to establish small cards as winners.

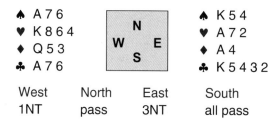

♠ A 7 6			♠ K 5 4
♥ K 8 6 4			♥ A 7 2
♦ Q 5 3			♦ A 4
♣ A 7 6			♣ K 5 4 3 2

West	North	East	South
1NT	pass	3NT	all pass

North leads ♠Q.

There are seven top winners and two more need to be established. You must look to clubs to provide, not just the two top winners, but two from East's small cards as well. Suppose, after winning the initial heart lead, you play ♣A and ♣K and note that both defenders follow suit. How many clubs are still around in enemy hands? Just one; you must lose to that card but, after that, only dummy (East) has any clubs left and they provide the two extra tricks that you require.

You can see that you are following a plan that is very similar to establishing tricks by driving out the defenders' top winners. Then you were establishing your other high cards. Here you are letting the defenders win one or more tricks to establish small cards in a long suit. In this example you, again, have no fear about giving up the lead because you know that it will be regained without danger.

Note, however, the advice given previously. Since you have to lose a club trick come what may, it is better technique to start by playing a small card from both hands as there will be more chance of changing direction later if a bad break is revealed.

♠ A K 6	N	♠ Q 5 4
♥ K 9 8 4	W E	♥ A 10
♦ Q 5 3	S	♦ A K 2
♣ 9 7 6		♣ 8 5 4 3 2

West plays in 3NT again. North leads ♠J.

Again, there are eight top winners and, despite its dearth of high cards, the club suit provides an excellent chance of establishing the ninth trick.

After winning the opening lead, you must immediately lead a club. It will lose, but you regain the lead and play a second club. That too will lose but, when you get the lead back, you play a third club. A long haul, but, at the end of the road, two of East's small clubs will have become established as winners given the expected 3-2 division of the defenders' cards.

This line of play is not certain to bring home the contract, but, with no help from the defence, it is the only chance to establish that vital ninth trick.

As with establishing top winners, you must establish small cards as winners before cashing your sure tricks in the other suits.

amending the odds

When you are declarer, you should take account of all the information that is available to you. This book is about play and not bidding and so far we have assumed that your opponents have not bid. However, if they do, they are giving you information, which you should use if you become declarer. If a defender has bid a suit, he will hold at least four cards in it. This may warn you to amend the odds of the theoretical distribution.

We will be looking at the significance of the opening lead later but, again, it can provide information that may cause you to change direction. If a defender leads a card in a suit from which you would otherwise be hoping to establish small cards as winners, you should be alert to the fact that it may not break as you hope. Defenders tend to lead from a long suit against a no trump contract.

Be alert to the rank of a card played by a defender. You were hoping to make four tricks from this combination:

A K 4 3 2	6 5

and, correctly, you start with a small card from West. If North follows with the jack (an unexpectedly high card), do not expect the suit to divide 3-3.

how small is small?

In the context of establishing tricks, a small card is one that can win a trick only when the opponents are unable to follow suit. This is in contrast to cards whose rank enables them to be or become top winners. The ten, for example, might be either. When supported by higher cards (e.g. Q J 10) it would be regarded as a high card but, if unsupported (e.g. 10 4 3 2), as a small card. Nevertheless, tens and nines in a hand are better than threes and twos, particularly since they act as barriers when the defence attacks a suit.

counting

It is important to count your potential tricks before you start to play. It is equally important to count the cards during the play, as well as noting whether a defender follows suit or not. This is a difficult, but important, discipline to cultivate, particularly since more than one suit may be involved.

You can start from a base of 13 and deduct the number of cards played in a particular suit on each round. Some find this a perfectly satisfactory method. Other declarers find it easier to start by deducting the combined (the declarer and dummy hands) number of cards held in each suit from 13 to give a total held by the opponents. This gives a lower base figure and makes calculating the probable split easier. For example, East-West have eight diamonds and, therefore, North-South have five. If North and South both follow suit to one round, you deduct a further two, leaving a combined total of three that are outstanding in their hands.

Counting is important – but difficult! The sooner you begin, the quicker you will develop the knack.

quiz

a) How many small cards might be established as winners from each of the given suit combinations?

b) How would you play the suit?

A K 3 2 5 4	a)	None. The ace and king are the only certain tricks.
	b)	Only cash the top winners when you have established any extra tricks required in other suits.
A K Q 2 5 4	a)	None. You can win only the ace, king and queen.
	b)	Delay taking your winners if you have tricks to establish elsewhere. A defender with four cards might, mistakenly, discard one when unable to follow to another suit.
A K Q 2 5 4 3	a)	One. The two might become a winner if the defenders' cards divide 3-3.
	b)	Delay cashing the three top winners. A defender with four cards might discard one in the earlier play.
A K 6 2 5 4 3	a)	One. About one third of the time the defenders' cards will divide 3-3.
	b)	Start with a small card from both hands. A trick must be lost in the suit and you should give it up at the start. This keeps entries to the West

hand and, by retaining the top winners, you control the suit and might be able to change your plan if, for example, a defender discards on the second round of the suit.

A 7 6 2	5 4 3	

a) One. An extra trick might be established in this suit. You would have to lose the lead twice and hope that the suit divides 3-3.

b) In the context of the overall hand, it is likely that there will be a better plan but, if needs must, you should play a small card from both hands twice, then play the ace and hope the suit divides 3-3.

8 7 6 5	4 3 2	

a) One, provided the defenders' cards split 3-3.

b) It is almost certain that you would not choose to lead this suit. However, you should be aware of its potential. Say the defenders cashed A K Q and both followed suit. West's fourth card would be established as a winner.

A 8 7 6	5 4 3 2	

a) One, provided two tricks can be given up.

b) Play small from both hands twice, then play the ace.

9 8 7 3	6 5 4 2	

a) One, provided three tricks can be given up.

b) Play the suit three times. The suit has a definite value because, with the probable 3-2 split, the defenders will be unable to take more than three tricks in it. If they choose to cash them, they will establish a trick for declarer.

A 8 7 6 5 4 3 2	a) Two, provided two tricks can be given up. Note that, as was shown earlier, when you hold eight cards in a suit, the defenders' cards will split 3-2 almost seven times out of ten. b) Play small from both hands twice, then the ace.
A K 8 7 6 5 4 3 2	a) Three, provided the defenders' cards split 2-2. b) Cash A and K. With nine cards in a suit there is a 50% chance that the other four divide 2-2 and produce five tricks. The suit is almost certain to be good for four tricks.
10 9 8 7 6 5 4 3 2	a) Three. Even without any top winners, that 50% chance of a 2-2 split would produce three tricks. b) Lead the suit twice establishing three small cards, if the suit divides 2-2. If a defender discards on the second round, you would still be able to establish two small cards by playing it a third time.

7 entries and blockages

It is no use having established winners unless you have an entry to get to them. Look at this hand:

	♠ A Q			♠ K J 10 3 2
	♥ A K 6 4 2	N		♥ 8 7
	♦ 6 5 3	W E		♦ A 4
	♣ A 7 3	S		♣ 9 8 6 5

West	North	East	South
1♥	pass	1♠	pass
2NT	pass	3♣	pass
3NT	all pass		

North leads ♦Q.

With a different lead, the contract would have been foolproof. West could cash ♠A and ♠Q and enter dummy with ♦A. There would be five certain spade tricks to go with the other four top winners. Now, that important diamond entry is about to disappear, if not immediately (East's ♦A need not be played at once), then at trick two.

Chances are still very good, however. After winning ♦A, you play ♠2 to ♠A and then ♠Q and overtake it with ♠K (the only certain way to win the lead back in dummy). If both defenders follow to this trick, you are safely home. East's remaining ♠J 10 are certain winners and, since, when they are cashed, nobody except dummy has any spades left, so is ♠3. On this hand, a top winner has to be sacrificed in the cause of gaining an entry to the small card winners.

How about this, in the same contract and with the same lead:

♠ A Q
♥ A K 6 4
♦ 6 5 3
♣ A 7 3 2

♠ K J 5 3 2
♥ 8 7
♦ A 4
♣ 9 8 6 5

After the diamond lead removes the vital ♦A entry, prospects are not so good as in the previous example, but they are not hopeless.

You still need to make five spade tricks and, again, after winning the ♦A, you must play to your ♠A and continue with the ♠Q and overtake it with dummy's ♠K. Although you know that is against the odds, this time you must hope that the six spades held by the defence divide 3-3 so that, when you now play ♠J, both defenders follow suit and, being the only cards outstanding in the suit, ♠5 and ♠3 are both winners.

Reject any thought of playing off ♠A and ♠Q thinking that a defender who wins the lead might oblige by playing another spade. Sometimes help comes from the enemy but do not expect an opponent to be that kind!

You might have considered that the club suit could produce two tricks and, in due course, an entry to dummy as well. However, this would mean having to lose two tricks in clubs and you are also destined to lose at least three diamonds as soon as the lead is lost.

There is another hazard, in the matter of entries, which is often appreciated only when it is too late. We warned earlier against 'blocking' a suit in this kind of situation:

A Q 4   K 2

Playing the ace before the king means that the queen is isolated. Blockages can happen in less obvious cases.

A 9 8 2	K Q 5 4 3

If this suit were hearts or spades it would probably be trumps. So it's likely to be clubs or diamonds when we play in no trumps.

We saw earlier that, when four cards are outstanding, they will divide 4-0 only one time in ten. This example, therefore, looks good to make five tricks.

But ... suppose West starts with the ace, both defenders following, and then the two towards East's holding and one defender shows out? We have a blockage here. East's second top winner must be played, in order to eliminate the last card held by the other defender, West's nine will be a fourth trick in the suit but East's last winner cannot be taken unless there is an outside entry to the East hand.

Due care would have avoided the problem. West's two must be preserved to avoid blocking the suit. After the ace is cashed, it must be the eight or nine that is led and the second blocking card must be played on East's second top winner.

We can make things really difficult:

A 9 8 7	K Q 5 4 3

Many declarers would mentally count this suit for five tricks when making their initial plan. If there is no outside entry in the East hand, it is in fact only a 50% chance since the suit will have to break 2-2 to be sure of five tricks. Can you see why?

The high spot cards in West's hand are the problem, forcing him to win the fourth trick in that hand if the suit breaks 3-1. If he has no outside entry he cannot get back to East to take the last diamond.

Let's put the suit into a context where declarer can find a solution, but only if he recognises the problem.

♠ A K	**N**	♠ 8 7 5
♥ A J 6 3	**W E**	♥ 8 4 2
♦ A 9 8 7	**S**	♦ K Q 5 4 3
♣ A 8 2		♣ J 4

West	North	East	South
2NT	pass	3NT	all pass

North leads ♠3 and South plays ♠Q.

There are seven top winners and, therefore, the diamond suit needs to provide two more. The problem is that it is blocked. Assume North holds, at most, five spades and try to find the way that declarer solved the problem before reading on.

West won the opening lead, perforce, and recognised that there might be a problem in making five diamond tricks. To overcome it, he first cashed the second top spade winner in his hand. Then he played ♦A and another to ♦Q. Had the suit divided 2-2, he would have been able to win the next diamond in the West hand to play his last diamond to East's ♦K 5.

However, North discarded on the second diamond lead. Declarer overcame this problem by playing East's ♠8 and discarding a diamond from hand. North was welcome to cash three spade tricks before the lead was regained. In the meantime, the diamond suit had been unblocked and the lone diamond left in West's hand gave the entry to East's winners.

It was a clever, but logical, play. As West, you would get a great deal of satisfaction from finding it.

When you count sure or likely tricks, double-check that a potential blockage will not prevent you from taking them.

8 giving up the lead

To establish tricks, whether top winners or small cards, you usually have to give up the lead. Declarers are often nervous of doing this even though – as in the hands that have been given so far – there is no danger in so doing. There are, however, some hands on which it is necessary to lose the lead and there is some danger in doing so. After all, it is no use establishing nine tricks in a 3NT contract if the defenders are able to take five tricks before you can cash them.

There are techniques to help us recognise and counteract the danger, which we will look at soon. For the moment let's look at some suit holdings which are not normally sources of tricks but which stop the opponents cashing all the tricks in the suit.

Here are three such suit holdings that offer this protection. They do not include certain winners but they do include cards which can hold off an attack by the enemy. Their value is easier to remember than to work out.

Q 2   J 4 3

Although this holding looks vulnerable, it cannot be played by the defence without giving you a trick in it. On the lead of a low card by either defender, you play small from the next hand giving the second defender the option of winning with the ace or king (leaving you with Q opposite J 4) or allowing you to win that trick with the queen or jack.

K 2   4 3

An unsupported king is a protection against the defence running the suit, but only if the hand to its left is on lead – that is provided the hand with the king is last to play to the trick. If the king is second to play, it can be beaten by the ace.

This holding in either declarer's hand or dummy's is more fragile but offers certain temporary protection. This is because, however the key cards are divided, the defenders cannot take more than two tricks in the suit at one go.

Take a little time to appreciate the reason. The key cards that you have to consider are the ace, queen and jack. Place them how you will with either defender on lead. If the hand with K 10 2 is last to play, the king is destined to win now or later. If the hand with K 10 2 is the second to play (e.g. South leads through West's holding), you simply play a higher card than the one led. If a small card is led, play the ten. If the queen or jack is led, play the king. In both cases the next defender will probably win the trick, but cannot continue the suit immediately without giving you a trick. In the first situation, you retain K 2 and are last to play to the next trick. In the second situation, you retain 10 2 and are, again, last to play, with the ace and either the queen or the jack already accounted for. Put the cards out and see how it works.

Note that, while you have breathing space, that is all it may be. A defender with A Q J 5 over your K 10 2 will probably prefer to hope that partner can regain the lead to play this suit once more.

Here are two examples, which show the importance of these holdings.

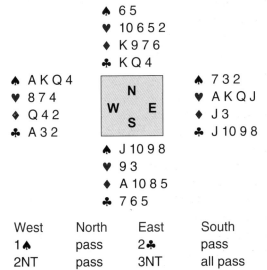

```
                   ♠ 6 5
                   ♥ 10 6 5 2
                   ♦ K 9 7 6
                   ♣ K Q 4
    ♠ A K Q 4          N           ♠ 7 3 2
    ♥ 8 7 4       W        E       ♥ A K Q J
    ♦ Q 4 2           S           ♦ J 3
    ♣ A 3 2                        ♣ J 10 9 8
                   ♠ J 10 9 8
                   ♥ 9 3
                   ♦ A 10 8 5
                   ♣ 7 6 5
```

West	North	East	South
1♠	pass	2♣	pass
2NT	pass	3NT	all pass

North leads ♥2.

When this hand was played, West failed to make the contract for no good reason other than the fact that he was afraid to lose the lead. He took his eight top winners in the hope that a 3-3 break in spades would produce the ninth. He worried, needlessly, about the diamonds. With eight certain tricks, he could have established the extra one in clubs. He must play ♣A on the second round of clubs, then a small club to avoid being cut off from the fourth club. If either defender led a diamond, the extra trick required would have been presented to him.

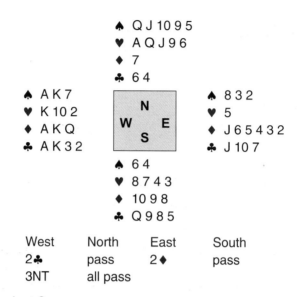

♠ Q J 10 9 5
♥ A Q J 9 6
♦ 7
♣ 6 4

♠ A K 7
♥ K 10 2
♦ A K Q
♣ A K 3 2

♠ 8 3 2
♥ 5
♦ J 6 5 4 3 2
♣ J 10 7

♠ 6 4
♥ 8 7 4 3
♦ 10 9 8
♣ Q 9 8 5

West	North	East	South
2♣	pass	2♦	pass
3NT	all pass		

North leads ♠Q.

After the opening lead, the contract is fireproof. West wins and cashes the A K Q of diamonds and then plays a small club towards dummy's ♣10 to ensure an entry to cash the long diamonds. A club has to be lost to the ♣Q (establishing East's ♣J) but West's ♥K 10 2 gives him the vital protection in that suit and the time needed to establish that entry in clubs. And, yes, West was lucky that North did not choose to lead a heart originally.

9 the finesse

Look at this hand or better still, make it up with a pack of cards.

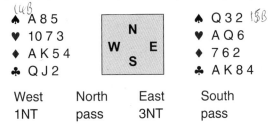

♠ A 8 5 (4B)
♥ 10 7 3
♦ A K 5 4
♣ Q J 2

♠ Q 3 2 15B
♥ A Q 6
♦ 7 6 2
♣ A K 8 4

West	North	East	South
1NT	pass	3NT	pass

North leads ♠J. You try ♠Q but South plays ♠K. You play low and South returns ♠4 and you win ♠A. Now you must take nine tricks without losing the lead as the opponents have all the spades to cash.

You have eight top tricks, so need to find one more trick. You have seven cards in diamonds but even if the defenders' diamonds break 3-3, the fourth diamond cannot be set up without losing the lead.

There is another chance. What about that ♥Q? It is no use leading out ♥A then ♥Q. They will just play low on the ace then kill the queen with the king.

There is another way you might be able to win a trick with ♥Q. If you lead a small card from West you do not have to decide which card to play from East until after North has decided which card to play. If he rises with ♥K, take the trick with ♥A and the queen is a winner for the ninth trick. If he plays low, play ♥Q and that is the vital extra trick.

Of course, if South has ♥K, this play will not work, but all things being equal, it's even money whether North or South holds the key card, ♥K.

This play is called a finesse and it comes in many forms, but they all involve making a hopeful assumption that a critical card is held by a particular defender.

Here is another example of a finesse:

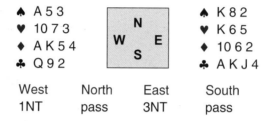

♠ A 5 3
♥ 10 7 3
♦ A K 5 4
♣ Q 9 2

♠ K 8 2
♥ K 6 5
♦ 10 6 2
♣ A K J 4

West	North	East	South
1NT	pass	3NT	pass

North leads ♠Q.

Again, there are eight top tricks. The diamonds might break 3-3, but they are more likely to be 4-2. An alternative, 50% shot is to finesse ♥A. Lead a small card towards ♥K and pray North has ♥A. The ♥K becomes a winner if North plays ♥A. If he holds up his ♥A, ♥K takes the trick.

Here are some more finesse positions. Work out how to play the cards to give yourself the best chance of making the number of tricks needed.

West	East	Tricks needed	What do you hope?
♥ K Q 2	♥ 4 3	2	South holds the ♥A

Play from East towards ♥ K Q 2. If the queen holds, return to dummy in another suit to lead a second time towards ♥ K 2.

West	East	Tricks needed	What do you hope?
♥ A K J 2	♥ 5 4 3	3	South holds the ♥Q

Play small from East and put in ♥J, if South plays low. You make three tricks if ♥J holds and four tricks if, additionally, the suit breaks 3-3.

West	East	Tricks needed	What do you hope?
♥ Q 10 9 7	♥ 6 5 4	1 or 2	South holds the ♥J

Lead small from East and play the nine or ten, if South plays low. If South has the jack, this will force the ace or king from North and, subsequently, another small card is led from East and the finesse is repeated. The queen will now make a trick and there is a chance of a second if either the suit divides 3-3 or South started with ♥ A J 8 3 or ♥ K J 8 3, and you are able to play yet a third time from East.

West	East	Tricks needed	What do you hope?
♥ A 4 3	♥ Q 2	2	North holds the ♥K

Lead the three from West towards ♥ Q 2. Either North will play the king and make both the ace and queen winners, or play small and the queen will hold the trick.

West	East	Tricks needed	What do you hope?
♥ Q J 2	♥ 7 3	1	South has an honour

Lead from East and play the jack if South plays low. If North wins, you play a second time from East towards ♥ Q 2. You make a trick when the ace and king are in separate hands or when South holds both.

West	East	Tricks needed	What do you hope?
♥ A J 10 4	♥ 3 2	2	South has one of the missing honours

Lead from East and play the ten, unless South puts up the king or queen. If North wins, you again play from East towards the ♥ A J 4. You make two tricks whenever the king and queen are in separate hands. You may even make three tricks if South holds exactly K Q or K Q x.

West	East	Tricks needed	What do you hope?
♥ K J 10 3	♥ 6 4 2	2	South holds the queen

Lead from East and play the ten, if South plays low. If North wins with the ace, then lead again towards ♥ K J and play the jack.

♥ A Q 10	♥ 3 2	2	Either the ♥K or ♥J or both are with South

Lead from East and play the ten. If it loses to North's jack, take a second finesse by leading towards ♥A Q. If you need three tricks play the same way but now you need South to hold ♥ K J.

These are just a few of many possible finesse positions. Do not try to learn them by heart! Just make sure you understand the general principle and you can work out what to do.

Play a small card towards the holding in the opposite hand, which you hope will win a trick either now or later.

Let's look in more detail at one example from the quiz above:

♥ A 4 3	♥ Q 2

Inexperienced players will sometimes try leading the queen hoping that, if South has the king, he won't play it, as he obviously should to prevent two tricks being made in the suit. It is foolish to hope that South will make a mistake in preference to the 50% chance that North has the king.

The following holdings are different because you have the next cards in the sequence.

♥ Q J 10	♥ A 3 2

You hope North holds the king. You can then make three tricks by leading the queen and letting it run if North plays low. Then you repeat the process with the jack. If the finesse loses, you will still have set up a second trick in the suit.

♥ J 10 9	♥ A 3 2

You must hope North has one of the missing honours. Start with ♥J, letting it run unless it is covered. Subsequently, you will play ♥10 from West and repeat the process. You make two tricks if North has the king or queen or both.

the two-way finesse

There are some holdings where you have the choice of playing for either defender to hold a key card. This will almost always involve a missing queen.

♥ A J 3 2	♥ K 10 5 4

Here, you have a choice to play for either defender to hold the queen. You could lead from West, and put in the ten, or from East and play the jack. With no other factors involved, it is a toss up which you do, but we will see that your decision may be affected by the fact that, if you have to lose a trick in the suit, you want to lose it to one particular defender (see Chapter 15).

Having made your choice of which opponent you want to hold the queen, can you see a small extra chance of making four tricks? If you hope that North holds the queen, start by leading the ace from West. South might hold the queen alone (a 'singleton') and now you have four tricks, come what may. Similarly, if you are going to play for South to hold the queen, start with the king in case North holds the singleton queen.

Here is an example that would determine how you played a two-way finesse:

	♠ 4 3 2			♠ 9 8 6
	♥ A K Q	**N**		♥ J 10 9
	♦ A J 3 2	**W E**		♦ K 10 5 4
	♣ A K 2	**S**		♣ Q 6 5

West	North	East	South
2NT	pass	3NT	all pass

North leads ♠A, ♠K and ♠Q (South follows suit) and then ♥8. How should you play 3NT?

Who has ♠J? Obviously South, otherwise North would have cashed that as well. There are eight top winners and the extra one can be established in diamonds, even if a trick is lost to the queen. However, if a trick is lost, it must not be South who takes it. He's got that ♠J, which would be the fifth trick for the defence. North, however, has no more spades and it is safe to lose the lead to his hand.

Therefore, after winning the fourth trick, declarer plays ♦2 to East's ♦K and then ♦4 to ♦J, if South does not produce ♦Q.

A finesse position can be held in reserve.

Look at possible finesse holdings when you make your initial plan.

Where did declarer go astray on this hand?

♠ A 4	N	♠ 7 6 2
♥ A K Q	W　　E	♥ J 10 3
♦ K Q 4 3 2	S	♦ A 7 5
♣ A 4 3		♣ Q J 5 2

West	North	East	South
2NT	pass	3NT	all pass

North leads ♠K.

From West's viewpoint, it all looked straightforward. He won the first trick and, being well versed in the good odds that the diamond suit would produce five tricks and in the technique of starting with the top winner in the shorter hand, he led ♦2 to dummy's ♦A and then ♦5 back to ♦KQ in hand. He confidently anticipated making five diamond tricks and ten in all. That is not how the play turned out. This was the full deal:

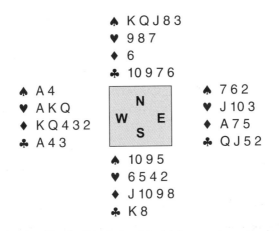

```
              ♠ K Q J 8 3
              ♥ 9 8 7
              ♦ 6
              ♣ 10 9 7 6
  ♠ A 4                        ♠ 7 6 2
  ♥ A K Q        N            ♥ J 10 3
  ♦ K Q 4 3 2  W   E          ♦ A 7 5
  ♣ A 4 3        S            ♣ Q J 5 2
              ♠ 10 9 5
              ♥ 6 5 4 2
              ♦ J 10 9 8
              ♣ K 8
```

The suit that had looked safe for five tricks produced only three
and there was no rescue available: eight tricks were the limit with
the defence waiting to cash four spade tricks as soon as they got
the lead. West was right to expect five tricks in diamonds but, if
that failed, there was the chance that clubs could produce two. At
trick two, he should have played a top diamond from West
followed by a small diamond to East's ♦A. The bad break would
come to light enabling declarer to resort to the alternative plan of
hoping that South held ♣K. Therefore, at trick four, he would play
East's ♣Q and let it run, if South failed to cover. If South held ♣K
(it does not matter how many cards are behind it), West must
make two club tricks and they will be enough to make the contract.

Recognise a potential finesse when you are making that essential
plan at the outset. You may need to rely on it or, as in our last
example, it may be a backstop.

when not to finesse

A finesse is a clever way of making a trick even when one of the
defenders holds a higher card in a suit. But don't get carried
away. There are times when it is unwise to finesse even though
you can.

One factor to bear in mind is that, unless there is other evidence from the defenders' bidding or play to date, a finesse only ever has a 50% chance of working. There is an old saying in bridge, 'eight ever, nine never'. It refers to whether you should take a finesse against a queen. If you have eight cards in a suit, for example:

♥ A K J 10 7   ♥ 8 3 2

You could play out the ace and king and hope the queen falls or you could try the finesse. Either or both might work on any particular hand but in the long run the best plan is to play with the odds. For the drop to work the opponents cards have to divide 3-2 with the queen as one of the cards in the doubleton. The chances of this happening are less than 50% so the finesse offers better prospects of success.

On the other hand, if you have nine cards:

♥ A K J 10 7 5   ♥ 8 3 2

The chances of dropping the queen have improved to over 50%, so just playing out the ace and king and hoping the queen falls offers a better chance of not losing a trick to the queen than the finesse.

Another time to refuse a possible finesse is when the player who will gain the lead if the finesse loses can threaten your contract.

♠ A K 5
♥ A 6 3
♦ K J 2
♣ A K 8 7

♠ Q 9 2
♥ 8 2
♦ A 9 8 7 3
♣ 9 5 3

West	North	East	South
2NT	pass	3NT	pass

North leads ♥K.

How should West plan the play?

There are eight top tricks, so West has to find one more. The diamonds must be able to produce that trick. Should declarer go for the finesse?

The danger here is the heart suit that North is trying to set up by leading ♥K. The first thing to do is to refuse to part with ♥A until South has run out of hearts. So let North have a couple of heart tricks and don't play the ♥A until the third trick. (See Chapter 14 for more about this 'hold up' play.) The other point is that the finesse can only be taken through South. If it loses, North gains the lead and he has a good heart suit just waiting to take lots of tricks. West has to play against the odds this time and hope North's ♦Q falls if he plays out the ace and king or that South has ♦Q. He will win but cannot continue the attack on hearts.

The full deal was:

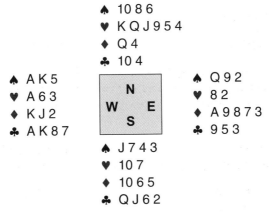

```
              ♠ 10 8 6
              ♥ K Q J 9 5 4
              ♦ Q 4
              ♣ 10 4
♠ A K 5                        ♠ Q 9 2
♥ A 6 3          N             ♥ 8 2
♦ K J 2      W       E         ♦ A 9 8 7 3
♣ A K 8 7        S             ♣ 9 5 3
              ♠ J 7 4 3
              ♥ 10 7
              ♦ 10 6 5
              ♣ Q J 6 2
```

If declarer takes the finesse against ♦Q, it fails and he goes down. If he plays against the odds, it works and he makes his contract with two overtricks. There are no such words as always and never in bridge!

How would you plan to play this hand?

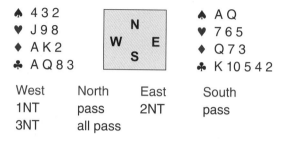

♠ 4 3 2
♥ J 9 8
♦ A K 2
♣ A Q 8 3

♠ A Q
♥ 7 6 5
♦ Q 7 3
♣ K 10 5 4 2

West	North	East	South
1NT	pass	2NT	pass
3NT	all pass		

North leads ♠6.

The chance to take a finesse should not distract you from a good reason for refusing to take it. North may well hold ♠K but, if South has it, you are in danger. If South has ♠K and is allowed to win the first trick, he may well switch to hearts, a suit in which at least four tricks are likely to be lost.

Play ♠A at trick one and rely on the club suit to be good for five tricks. One other thing to note here when playing the clubs. Cash ♣A. Should South show out, cash ♣Q and play a small club towards ♣K 10. You then know North has ♣J so this is a 'marked finesse'. This is another example of keeping a finesse position in reserve in case you need it.

You don't have to take a finesse just because it's there! Refuse it when:

- The bidding or play so far suggests it will fail anyway.

- When it is against the odds.

- When one defender can gain the lead and threaten the contract if the finesse fails.

quiz on the finesse

♠ A 9 4　　　　　　　　　　　　♠ 7 6 2
♥ Q 10 3　　　　　 N 　　　　　♥ 9 8 6
♦ A Q J 3　　 W 　　 E 　　　♦ K 7 5
♣ 6 4 3　　　　　　 S 　　　　♣ A Q 8 2

West opens 1NT and everybody passes. North leads ♥5 to South's ♥A and South returns ♥7. North wins ♥J and cashes ♥K and two more hearts before playing ♠J. West has only lost five tricks but the defence now have good spades to cash. Can you find a way to take seven tricks?

One spade, four diamonds and a club is six tricks. The club finesse is the only chance for one more. Win the spade, cash four diamond tricks and play ♣3. When North plays low, play ♣Q from dummy and hope that North holds ♣K.

♠ A 9 4　　　　　　　　　　　　♠ 7 6
♥ A 8 3　　　　　 N 　　　　　♥ K 9 6
♦ 4 3 2　　　 W 　　 E 　　　♦ A J 10 9
♣ A J 10 3　　　　　 S 　　　♣ K Q 5 2

West's 1NT is raised to 3NT and North leads ♥4. How should West play to get nine tricks?

West must win the heart, as a spade switch would be damaging. With only eight top tricks, diamonds offer the best chance of a ninth. Win ♥A and play ♦2. If North plays low, put in ♦9 from dummy. If it loses, win the heart return and cross to West with a club. Play another diamond and if North plays low, play ♦10. West will make 3NT if North has one or both diamond honours. In any case one diamond winner must get set up and there is the extra chance that hearts break 4-3 and only two heart tricks are lost.

```
    ♠ A 4 3                    ♠ K 6 2
    ♥ K Q 7        N           ♥ A J 10
    ♦ Q 4 3     W     E        ♦ A 7 5 2
    ♣ A 7 4 3      S           ♣ K 5 2
```

West's 1NT is raised to 3NT and North leads ♣Q, South discarding ♥2. How should West play?

West has eight top tricks. One chance for a ninth was a 3-3 club break and that is clearly not happening. There is no point in ducking the club, so win ♣A and play ♦3 to ♦A. Now lead ♦2. 3NT will make if South has ♦K or it is singleton with North.

```
    ♠ A 8                      ♠ K Q 4
    ♥ 7 5 3        N           ♥ A 9 2
    ♦ Q J 10    W     E        ♦ A 9 8 6 4
    ♣ A Q J 10 4   S           ♣ 3 2
```

Against West's 3NT North leads ♥K. You decide not to win your ♥A until trick three – remember you don't have to win a trick just because you can. On the third trick South throws a small spade. How do you continue?

You can finesse in clubs or diamonds. But if the club finesse loses, North has two hearts to cash. Come to hand with ♠A and lead ♦Q. Play low from dummy unless North produces the king. If South wins he can do you no harm with the return and you will make three spades, one heart, four diamonds and a club.

10 combining all the chances

We have looked at three different ways of making extra tricks when the initial count of the sure, or probable, tricks is insufficient.

- Driving out the defenders' top winners to establish top winners for declarer.

- Establishing small cards as winners because all the defenders cards have been played and the small cards have become winners.

- Making an assumption that a key card is with a particular defender and taking a finesse.

As declarer, you will often have to choose which option to pursue.

```
        ♠ A 4 2              ♠ K Q 3
        ♥ Q 4         N      ♥ J 10 9 6
        ♦ A 4 3 2   W   E    ♦ K 8 7 5
        ♣ K J 6 3     S      ♣ A 5
```

West	North	East	South
1NT	pass	2♣	pass
2♦	pass	3NT	all pass

North leads ♠J.

As always, make your plan before you touch a single card.

You can see seven sure winners – three spades, two diamonds and two clubs.

What opportunities are there to set up those extra two tricks? Diamonds could provide one, if the suit breaks 3-2. Clubs could provide one, if South holds ♣Q, by taking a finesse. Combining these two options would give you the two tricks needed about one time in three.

Hearts, however, can provide both tricks all of the time. You will have to lose the lead twice to establish those tricks, but there is no danger in doing so. After winning the first trick with ♠A, you have two further spade stoppers and no switch can hurt you.

There will be no problem in cashing the heart winners when you have set them up, as you have plenty of entries to the East hand. So it's clear you should play on hearts at trick two. Change the hands slightly to get:

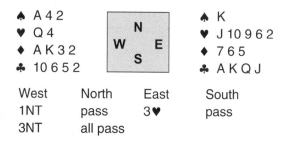

	♠ A 4 2			♠ K
♥ Q 4			♥ J 10 9 6 2
♦ A K 3 2			♦ 7 6 5
♣ 10 6 5 2			♣ A K Q J

West	North	East	South
1NT	pass	3♥	pass
3NT	all pass		

North leads ♠Q.

It looks quite like the last problem, but it isn't. You have eight sure tricks and need just one more. Hearts could provide not just one but three extra tricks by driving out ♥A and ♥K.

But is there any danger in playing on hearts? Unfortunately there is. The lead must be lost twice to establish those tricks. The defence will establish their spade winners when they get in with the first heart and they will cash them when they get in with the second. At best, you will lose three spades as well as the two top winners in hearts.

Is there an alternative? If a diamond is ducked and if the diamonds break 3-3, then a small diamond in West's hand will be established as a winner. This is against the odds but it will mean losing the lead only once and that's all right as you have a second spade stopper.

Remember the defenders can only see dummy and don't know that you have four diamonds. It won't do any harm to start by cashing the four top clubs. The defenders will have to discard and, maybe, if one of them has four diamonds, he will go wrong by discarding one.

Again the conclusion is clear, but very different – making three diamond tricks is the best chance. Win the opening lead, play the four top clubs and then a small diamond from both hands. The next hand offers a choice of plays which, with care, can be combined.

♠ K 3 2		♠ A 5 4
♥ 8 7	N	♥ A 6 4
♦ 7 6 2	W E	♦ A Q J 5
♣ A K Q 5 4	S	♣ 9 8 2

West	North	East	South
1NT	pass	3NT	all pass

North leads ♥K.

Here we have seven top winners, two spades, two red aces and three top clubs, leaving two more to be found.

Which suits can provide two extra tricks? Diamonds might, but only if North holds ♦K, which he will do half the time. The diamond finesse can be taken twice as there are enough entries. However, clubs will provide two extra tricks if the suit splits 3-2 and that happens about two thirds of the time, so it is a better shot.

You cannot afford to lose the lead. The defence will cash their heart winners; certainly they have three, maybe four. So win ♥A and play West's three top clubs. If the clubs break 4-1, this will be revealed when the second top club is played. Now you can try your second chance – the diamond finesse. If it is successful, come back to hand with ♠K and repeat the finesse.

Careful thinking shows there is only one line on the next hand, even though at first sight there appears to be a choice.

```
    ♠ A 4 2              ♠ K 6 5
    ♥ Q 7         N      ♥ 8 6 5 2
    ♦ 7 6 2    W   E     ♦ A Q J 10
    ♣ A K Q 5 4    S     ♣ 9 8
```

West	North	East	South
1♣	pass	1♦	pass
1NT	pass	3NT	all pass

North leads ♠Q.

Now you only have six top winners. Three to find, and there is a real danger in losing the lead as the defence can certainly take at least four heart tricks.

Which suit can provide the extra three winners? Well, clubs look promising, but even if they divide 3-3 that is only two extra tricks. Only diamonds can give you those three extra tricks and that needs North to hold ♦K to be successful. So, despite the risk that South has ♦K, the diamond finesse must be taken immediately and if it works, it can be repeated twice more.

When thinking about the way to play a hand, ask yourself:

■ How many sure winners do I have?

■ How many extra tricks must I find?

■ Which suits can provide the extra tricks?

■ Is there a danger if I lose the lead?

■ Is there an alternative line of play? Which line of play offers me the best chance?

■ What is my plan?

11 understanding the opening lead

We hope that you have been persuaded that:

- When you need to establish extra tricks, it is likely that you have to give up the lead.

- You must establish those extra tricks as a priority, before cashing your certain winners.

We have deliberately shown this process taking place in a danger-free zone. We are now going to map out land where there may be pitfalls and, to avoid danger, the first necessity is to know where they may lie. An analysis of the opening lead made by the defence is particularly valuable.

Defensive technique is outside the scope of this book (see *Really Easy Defence*) but it is important to know some basic facts about how the enemy's campaign to defeat you starts with the opening lead.

Good defenders glean information about each other's hands from the cards they play. The process starts with the opening lead. However, neither in the bidding nor the play are partners allowed to have a secret understanding. Therefore any information that an opening lead provides to the other defender is equally available to declarer and he should make the best use of it.

As declarer you should, therefore, assume that a defender has a reason both for leading a certain suit and in selecting a particular card from that suit. There is, of course, no law that requires this code to be followed and deception is part of the game. But a defender who regularly tries to deceive, or who leads haphazardly, will cause more trouble for his partner than for declarer.

The opening lead against a no trump contract will either attack, seeking to establish tricks for the partnership, or defend, seeking not to give a trick away. When making an attacking lead, defender will have the same objective as declarer – establishing extra tricks. This may be by driving out the top winners in the opposing hands or by trying to establish small cards, in a long suit, as winners.

When there is a choice between the two objectives, leading a long suit against a no trump contract is likely to be the more productive. With Q J 10 in one suit and A K 4 3 2 in another, a defender will, almost certainly, choose the longer suit. It has the potential of establishing more tricks. Sometimes, the two objectives coincide – from Q J 10 3 2, the queen would start the process of driving out declarer's top winner(s) and the three and two might additionally become small card winners.

An attempt to establish tricks in partner's suit rather than his own would also be an attacking lead by a defender. Leading a suit that his partner has bid would be an example but, if the defender can see no likelihood of establishing tricks in his own hand, he may hope to find his partner with a long or strong suit.

A defensive (or 'passive') lead is likely to be made by a defender who has some unsupported high cards, but no suit to establish. He will hope that, when declarer has to initiate leading a key suit(s), tricks will materialise. If North held:

♠ J 10 9　♥ K J 3　♦ J 7 3 2　♣ Q 10 4

he might well choose the ♠J, which should give nothing away.

Once the defender making the opening lead has decided on the suit, the choice of which card is selected should conform to 'standard' practice. This means that, from certain suit holdings, a particular card is chosen. The objective is to provide information to the other defender, but it gives the same news to declarer.

standard leads

It is not easy to store these in the memory but recognising them will be very helpful in planning the play. The logic behind some can be understood but, with others, it may have to be taken on trust.

a high card is led

When a defender lacks the top winner(s) in a suit but has a sequence of three or more high cards, the top card should be led. The same top card should be led with two top cards in sequence, missing the next, but holding the following one.

For example:

- K from suits headed by K Q J or K Q 10

- Q from suits headed by Q J 10 or Q J 9

Therefore, if a queen is led initially, both declarer and the other defender are entitled to assume that the player on lead does not hold the king.

When a defender has one high card, with either one or both of the next two missing, but holds the next two in sequence, the top card in the interior sequence is chosen.

For example:

- Q from suits headed by A Q J

- J from suits headed by A J 10 or K J 10

The information provided, in these second examples, can be ambiguous since the queen would also be led from Q J 10 and the jack from J 10 9.

The probability is that, when one of these high cards is led, it is from a long suit and there are small cards with the top cards, which may become established as winners. This is not certain (queen from Q J 10 alone would be an excellent passive lead) but the danger is there and declarer should take account of it.

a small card is led

A small card will almost certainly be from a long suit in which the defender is hoping to establish small cards as winners. The defender won't have a sequence, which would be led in preference to a small card.

From a 4-card or longer suit, there is, again, a standard lead for the same purpose of providing information to partner. It is the fourth highest card in the suit counting from the top.

For example:

- 2 from A J 9 2

- 3 from A J 9 3 2

The rank of the card assists declarer. When the two is led, that defender should have only a 4-card suit. When the three is led, it should be from a 4-card suit if the two is on view in declarer's or dummy's hand. If not, it may be from a 5-card suit.

Let's look at a hand that we had earlier to see what information declarer could derive, knowing that the lead is the fourth highest. In this particular case, it is comforting rather than vital news since it will not change declarer's line of play.

	♠ K J 2			♠ Q 8 6
	♥ Q 10 9 2	**N**		♥ K J 3
	♦ K 10 2	**W** **E**		♦ Q 9 3
	♣ Q J 9	**S**		♣ K 10 8 2

West played in 2NT. North led ♠3 and we were confident that, despite the fact that there were no top winners available and tricks had to be established in all four suits, declarer would be successful.

Why such confidence? Consider that ♠3 lead, which is surely from a long suit. But how long? Assuming that it is the fourth highest, it can be only a 4-card suit because West can see the ♠2 in his own hand. It means that the defence will be able to take only two spade tricks (the ♠A and the lone thirteenth card in the suit which, in due course, will be established) to go with the other three aces.

When a defender initially leads a small card it is likely to be from a long suit.

Sometimes, the initial lead of a middle ranking card can be ambiguous. Is it from a long suit or from a short suit, being an attempt to find length or strength in the other defender's hand? The next chapter will help you identify it but, when this is not possible, it is probably better to assume that it is from a long suit.

Be clear that we are talking about the initial lead only. During the subsequent play, low cards may be led from 3-card suits. A good guideline is to assume that a small card will indicate that the defender who leads it holds an honour (A K Q J or 10) and a high card indicates that he holds no higher card in the suit.

12 the rule of eleven

The last chapter gave some general guidance for deducing information from the defenders' leads. Here is something precise.

There is a very simple but important rule that is particularly useful for the partner of the defender who makes the initial lead. We are going to look at the information that it can also provide to the declarer. This is how it works:

When the initial lead is, or may be, the fourth highest of a long suit, deduct the rank of the card led from eleven. The resulting figure tells you how many cards, higher than the one led, are in the other three hands. Once dummy is exposed, two of those hands are visible. Therefore, as declarer, you know how many of those higher cards are held by your right-hand opponent.

For example:

K 10 7   J 6 2

North leads the five. It looks like the fourth highest so West takes 5 from 11 = 6. Five of those six cards are visible, three with West and two with East. Therefore there is only one higher card in South's hand. A small card is played from dummy and, say, South plays the nine enabling West to win cheaply with the ten. This may look satisfactory but it's not particularly good news. That one higher card with South has been exposed and all the other higher cards (A Q 8 plus, probably, one or two smaller cards) must be in North's hand. West's K 7 still protects the suit if North is on lead but not if South is on lead.

Which is the one higher card that you wish had been played by South? The queen! You could then win the king and, holding both jack and ten, be certain that a second trick in the suit could be established.

10 4 2	A Q 3

North leads the eight of this suit.

This is a more important example. From the lead, West is not sure whether North has led from a long suit (e.g. K J 9 8 5) or from a short suit (e.g. 8 5). However, all will become clear after the play to the first trick.

The three should be played from East. Why? Because, as declarer, you subtract 8 from 11 = 3. All those three higher cards are visible and therefore, if the lead is the fourth highest, West's ten is high enough to win the first trick.

If West's ten is good enough, then the suit will produce three tricks since you can lead towards A Q and finesse in the knowledge that North holds the king. Suppose you had not done the arithmetic and decided to play the queen from dummy on the first trick, simply thinking that North was the more likely to hold the king? You would make two tricks but not three. North's K J would prevent the third.

Conversely, suppose North has led the top card from a doubleton 8 5, hoping to establish tricks in his partner's suit. South would now hold K J 9 7 4. When East's three is played South's jack would win the first trick. Then, however, South would be unable to lead the suit again without letting both the ace and queen in East's hand become winners. He would, no doubt, switch to another suit hoping that North can win and lead through dummy's A Q. This would not only give you time to go about establishing other tricks but, in so doing, you might be able to arrange it that South rather than North gets the lead.

It is true that, If North has led from 8 5, the play of East's queen would still prevent South from continuing the suit when he won the king, since West has 10 4 and East A 3. However, it gains nothing and loses that extra trick when North has led from a long suit.

The examples that have been given will probably be clearer if, as was suggested at the start of this book, you have a pack of cards available and can go through the play. For example, if you isolate any one suit and apportion it:

A Q 8 5 3
K 10 7   J 6 2
9 4

You will see that, when the first trick goes 5, 2, 9 and is won by West's 10, the lead of the four from South will allow North to win all four of his remaining cards. By giving South the queen and North the nine, you can understand how declarer can make two tricks.

Apply the Rule of Eleven before you play to the first trick.

quiz

a) What information about the suit led can you derive from the card selected as the opening lead?

b) How might this information influence your initial plan?

K led	a) Since the ace and jack are visible, the lead must be from a suit headed by K Q 10.
A 7 4 J 3 2	b) Win the ace at trick one. Subsequently, by leading towards East's J 3, a second trick will be made. North has been unlucky in his choice of opening lead.
J led	a) North holds neither the queen (the lead of the jack denies it), nor the ace (the only standard lead, holding both A and J, is from A J 10 and, here, West holds 10).
10 4 2 K 8 6	b) Cover with East's king. South will win the ace but West's 10 4 will make a trick provided the lead was from jack and another.
3 led	a) The lead is surely from a long suit.
A 8 7 Q 4	b) Play East's queen hoping that North holds the king. The only hope of making the queen is at trick one.
7 led	a) The lead is ambiguous. It could be from a long suit headed by Q J 8 7 or from a short suit, for example, 7 6.
10 9 2 A K 3	

b) If it's fourth highest, the Rule of Eleven (11 − 7 = 4) tells you that West will be able to win the trick. If you are a trick short, play small from East. If you see that, should South win the first trick, a lead of another suit spells danger, play safe.

6 led

A 9 2   K 10 3

a) Assume that the lead is the fourth highest, but the play at trick one is unaffected.

b) The Rule of Eleven (11 − 6 = 5) means that South has only one card higher than the six. Play small from East and, if South produces the queen or jack, West wins the ace and there is a finesse position that produces two more tricks. The suit could be:

J 8 7 6 5
A 9 2   K 10 3
Q 4

5 led

A 6 2   Q J 9

a) Surely the fourth highest from a long suit.

b) By using the Rule of Eleven declarer can conclude that South has only one card higher than the five. Play the queen or jack from East and, should South cover with the king, West can win the ace and there is a sure finesse position for two more tricks.

13 have the defenders bid?

All four players are entitled to make bids and, when a defender has bid a suit, the declarer can use the information provided.

We will look at two examples.

```
        ♠ A 8 3 2          ┌─────────┐          ♠ Q 6
        ♥ 3                │    N    │          ♥ K J 9 6 4
        ♦ J 9 8 5          │ W     E │          ♦ K Q 10
        ♣ A Q 9 4          │    S    │          ♣ 6 3 2
                           └─────────┘
```

West	North	East	South
pass	1♣	1♥	pass
1NT	all pass		

North leads ♠4.

East's ♠Q should be played (it's now or never, if it is to win a trick) and South follows with ♠5. At trick two, East's ♦K is played to drive out ♦A. South wins this trick and leads ♣8 (the suit his partner bid).

Time to pause for a little counting. East-West started with a combined 22 points, so North-South have 18. ♦A shows South had four of them leaving 14 points. The opening bid suggests North has at least twelve of these. There can be at most only two points left in South's hand. So North must have both ♣K and ♥A.

There is no point in taking the club finesse since North is known to have ♣K. If West wins ♣A the ♣Q 9 4 will still protect the suit.

At this stage, declarer has made two tricks (♠Q and ♣A) and has ♠A to come and three diamond winners have been established.

Needing just one more trick, he should lead his lone heart, confidently playing East's ♥K if North plays low. This should be done before cashing the winning diamonds to be certain of an entry to dummy if North rises with ♥A when the ♥3 is led.

The full hand:

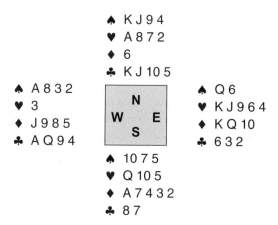

```
              ♠ K J 9 4
              ♥ A 8 7 2
              ♦ 6
              ♣ K J 10 5
♠ A 8 3 2                    ♠ Q 6
♥ 3              N           ♥ K J 9 6 4
♦ J 9 8 5    W      E        ♦ K Q 10
♣ A Q 9 4         S          ♣ 6 3 2
              ♠ 10 7 5
              ♥ Q 10 5
              ♦ A 7 4 3 2
              ♣ 8 7
```

North had a difficult lead but thought it more likely that South had the ♠A or ♠Q than either of the same honours in clubs, in which West's 1NT bid had indicated good cover.

The contract could still succeed, but South would have made things more difficult by holding up the ♦A until the third round.

The occasions on which you play a no trump contract after an opponent has opened the bidding are fairly rare. The second example is more subtle because the enemy has not made a bid!

```
          ♠ A 9 3                    ♠ K Q J
          ♥ 7 6 4          N          ♥ 10 9 8 2
          ♦ K 7 4 2     W     E       ♦ A Q 3
          ♣ A 10 9          S          ♣ K J 8
```

West	North	East	South
pass	pass	1♥	pass
2NT	pass	3NT	all pass

North leads ♥A and continues with ♥K, ♥Q and ♥J. He then leads ♠4.

The diamond suit may break 3-3 and, therefore, declarer starts by cashing the three top winners. When this fails, he has to resort to a finesse in clubs for the ninth trick.

North has shown ten points already and with ♣Q he would have twelve and would probably have opened the bidding. Assume South holds the ♣Q and play a club to the ten.

The full hand:

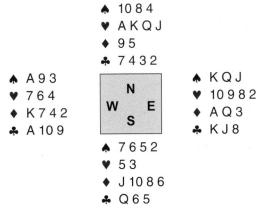

```
                    ♠ 10 8 4
                    ♥ A K Q J
                    ♦ 9 5
                    ♣ 7 4 3 2
     ♠ A 9 3                          ♠ K Q J
     ♥ 7 6 4            N             ♥ 10 9 8 2
     ♦ K 7 4 2       W     E          ♦ A Q 3
     ♣ A 10 9            S             ♣ K J 8
                    ♠ 7 6 5 2
                    ♥ 5 3
                    ♦ J 10 8 6
                    ♣ Q 6 5
```

North defended naively by displaying all his goods so quickly. A passive lead or a switch would give declarer a chance to go wrong.

Counting a defender's points can give a clue to the play.

quiz

Play 3NT on the lead of ♠9 after the auction

	♠ A K			♠ 8 4 2
	♥ K 7 4	**N**		♥ Q J 10
	♦ A 10 9 3	**W** **E**		♦ K J 7 2
	♣ K 9 5 4	**S**		♣ A 3 2

West	North	East	South
			1♠
1NT	pass	3NT	all pass

If you play on hearts, South wins ♥A and plays ♠Q.

You have two spades, two diamonds and two clubs. Playing hearts gives two more. Win the spade and drive out ♥A. South wins and plays ♠Q, removing your second stopper. E/W have a combined 28 points, so South needs all the missing points to make an opening bid. Play ♦K and lead ♦J. If South plays low, take the finesse and if need be repeat the finesse to make four diamond tricks.

Play 3NT on the lead of ♠Q after the auction

	♠ A K			♠ 8 4 2
	♥ K 7 4	**N**		♥ Q J 10
	♦ A 10 9 3	**W** **E**		♦ K J 7 2
	♣ K 9 5 4	**S**		♣ A 3 2

West	North	East	South
	1♠	pass	pass
1NT	pass	3NT	all pass

If you play on hearts, North wins ♥A and plays ♠J.

It's the same hand but this time North opened the bidding, not South. Drive out ♥A and win the spade return. This time it is North who must have the ♦Q, so play ♦A then the ♦10, finessing if North plays low.

Play 3NT on the lead of ♠K, South playing ♠7.

```
        ♠ A 10 9              ♠ 4 2
        ♥ K J 10 4     N      ♥ Q 5
        ♦ Q 3 2     W     E   ♦ A K J 9 8
        ♣ A 5 2        S      ♣ K J 10 4
```

West	North	East	South
	pass	1♦	pass
1♥	pass	2♣	pass
3NT	all pass		

Do not take ♠A straightaway. Not only will this cut the defenders' communication (see next chapter), it will also give you clues about the cards they hold. North continues with ♠Q and ♠J and South throws ♣6 on the third round of spades.

North could not open or overcall. Most players would bid with ♠K Q J 8 6 5 and ♥A. So don't try and guess who has ♣Q, just play on hearts and drive out ♥A. Of course if North has failed to bid when holding ♥A you will go down.

```
        ♠ J 4                ♠ Q 10 2
        ♥ K J 10       N     ♥ A 8 5
        ♦ A Q 10 7 6 W     E ♦ K J 4
        ♣ A 5 3        S     ♣ 9 6 4 2
```

West	North	East	South
	1♣	pass	pass
1NT	pass	3NT	all pass

♣K lead. South discards ♠7. You win the ♣A and cash the diamonds. North has three, then throws ♠9 and ♠3. South throws two small spades and ♥2.

North has six clubs and three diamonds. The ♠9 3 and the opening bid show North started with either ♠A 9 3 or ♠A K 9 3 so he cannot have more than one heart. After cashing the diamonds, play a heart to ♥A and if ♥Q has not appeared, play a heart to ♥J and finesse.

14 the hold-up play

In the battle to establish tricks, the defence has the advantage of being able to fire the first shot with the opening lead. Frequently, this will be from a long suit in which declarer may have inadequate protection.

The relatively good news is first that you can usually recognise the danger by diagnosing the lead and second that, if one hand has a dangerously long suit, his partner will be short in it. This may enable you to counter the attack.

The 'hold-up' technique is, probably, not just the most valuable manoeuvre that is available to a declarer in no trump contracts but also the one that is most frequently used. This is the logic:

You do not have to win a trick simply because you can. You can refuse to win it until you are forced to or until you want to.

It may seem odd to refuse to win a trick but, unless you are in a grand slam, the defenders will always win some tricks. Let them have them at a time to suit you, not them.

We said that, if one defender was dangerously long in a suit, his partner would be short in it. If you refuse to win a trick in the identified long suit until the point at which the other defender has no more cards left in it, your winning options are better because, if he gets the lead he will have to switch to another suit. This may give you a vital opportunity to establish extra tricks.

What you are doing, by holding off winning a trick that you could choose to win, is trying to cut the communications between the two defenders' hands.

Here is an example:

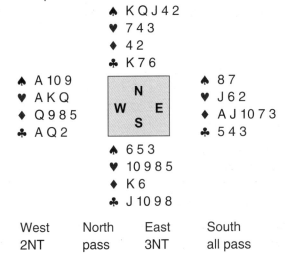

	♠ K Q J 4 2	
	♥ 7 4 3	
	♦ 4 2	
	♣ K 7 6	

♠ A 10 9		♠ 8 7
♥ A K Q	N	♥ J 6 2
♦ Q 9 8 5	W E	♦ A J 10 7 3
♣ A Q 2	S	♣ 5 4 3

	♠ 6 5 3	
	♥ 10 9 8 5	
	♦ K 6	
	♣ J 10 9 8	

| West | North | East | South |
| 2NT | pass | 3NT | all pass |

North leads ♠K.

Consider, as West, what would happen if you won the first trick with ♠A. You have to make some diamond tricks, and you can see a finesse position: if North holds ♦K, you will make all five diamonds. Accordingly, you lead ♦Q and, when North fails to cover with ♦K, you play ♦3 from East. Sadly, South wins ♦K and leads a spade and North wins all four of his remaining spades to put the contract down by one trick.

Now play it a different way.

The opening ♠K lead will be from a suit headed by K Q J or K Q 10. West has ♠10, so it must be from K Q J. There are likely to be small cards in addition.

Making a plan before playing any card, you see that extra winners must be made from diamonds and that this may involve losing the lead to South.

There is no need to win with West's ♠A at trick one. If you refuse to take the first trick, North retains the lead and a switch to another suit can do you no damage. So, on the first trick, you hold up ♠A. North will continue with ♠Q and, again, you refuse to part with ♠A. North will probably persist with a third spade, which finally drives out West's ace.

West's ♦Q is led with the intention of taking the finesse. It loses to ♦K, but South has run out of spades. North has two potential winners in the suit but, for the moment, has no means of making them.

There is one final decision to be made. With no spades left, South is obliged to play another suit after winning ♦K. Say he chooses ♣J. West's holding in this suit (A Q 2) is another finesse position. If South holds ♣K, you could make both ace and queen, but this finesse must be rejected. By now you are sure of nine tricks (one spade, three hearts, four diamonds and ♣A). You do not need to make two club tricks and it would be foolish to take the risk. Here, it would be fatal. North would win ♣K and happily cash those two established spade winners.

Winning ♠A, at tricks one or two, gives the contract a 50% chance since it depends on the location of ♦K. Holding up ♠A until trick three makes it 100%. If South produces a fourth spade, after winning ♦K, then North started with only four spades. The defence can then take only three spade tricks to go with ♦K.

On this occasion the hold-up play ensured the contract. But it is also correct technique when it depends on good luck to be successful.

Let's change our example slightly. The contract is still 3NT.

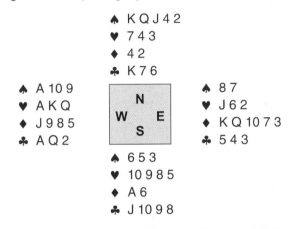

♠ K Q J 4 2
♥ 7 4 3
♦ 4 2
♣ K 7 6

♠ A 10 9
♥ A K Q
♦ J 9 8 5
♣ A Q 2

♠ 8 7
♥ J 6 2
♦ K Q 10 7 3
♣ 5 4 3

♠ 6 5 3
♥ 10 9 8 5
♦ A 6
♣ J 10 9 8

North leads ♠K and, once more, West needs to establish diamond tricks, this time by driving out ♦A.

Again, West must hold up ♠A until trick three. When he plays diamonds, South wins ♦A and, as before, has no more spades left to lead.

Here, you have to hope that the vital ♦A is where you want it. By luck, it is with South, the hand that can do you no harm. It could easily be with North and the defence would make five tricks. When this happens, blame the gods but not the way you played the hand. If you do not hold up ♠A, you would be defeated for certain, whoever had ♦A. By holding up, you give yourself a 50% chance of success.

How many rounds should you hold up? You can always work it out but some players like to use the Rule of Seven as a guide.

Add together the number of cards in dummy and declarer's hand. Subtract the answer from seven. The result is the number of rounds to hold up.

So in the hand above we have five cards in the suit led. 7 – 5 = 2, so we should hold up twice.

Most often, it will be the ace of a suit which needs to be held up since it is a certain trick, which can be taken whenever you want. However, it is possible for a king to take its place.

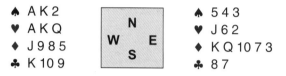

♠ A K 2   ♠ 5 4 3
♥ A K Q   ♥ J 6 2
♦ J 9 8 5   ♦ K Q 10 7 3
♣ K 10 9   ♣ 8 7

West is playing that 3NT contract again and this time North leads ♣3 on which South plays ♣A and returns ♣6. ♣K has now become a certain trick and, as such, should be withheld at trick two. No switch of suit is dangerous and the hold-up is being employed in the hope that South has only three clubs and that vital ♦ A.

Note that West could hold up ♣K only because South's ♣A had appeared and ♣K was then the top card. This is very different:

♠ A K 2   ♠ 5 4 3
♥ A K Q   ♥ J 6 2
♦ J 9 8 5   ♦ K Q 10 7 3
♣ K 10 9   ♣ 8 7

North again leads ♣3 but this time, South follows with ♣J. For sure, ♣K is a certain trick, but only if it is taken straight away, at trick one. If withheld, it may never be won. This is a likely distribution of the suit, taken in isolation:

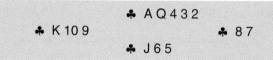

                ♣ A Q 4 3 2
♣ K 10 9   ♣ 8 7
                ♣ J 6 5

The king must be won immediately or consigned to the grave.

As for the contract? Well, it's looking pretty sick but it's not yet dead. All that is known, before the king has to be played on the first trick, is that North has led from a long suit which could contain either four or five cards. It may happen that it's a 4-card suit and this is the distribution:

♣ A Q 4 3

♣ K 10 9   ♣ 8 7

♣ J 6 5 2

Now the contract succeeds since only three club tricks will be lost.

In the interests of being absolutely honest, sometimes there's a defender too clever for our own good.

♠ Q 9 6
♥ 10 4 3
♦ 6 4
♣ Q 6 4 3 2

♠ A K 2   ♠ 5 4 3
♥ A K Q   ♥ J 6 2
♦ J 9 8 5   ♦ K Q 10 7 3
♣ K 10 9   ♣ 8 7

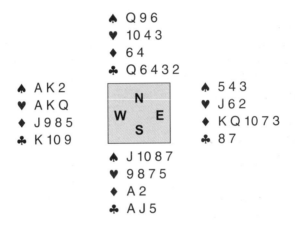

♠ J 10 8 7
♥ 9 8 7 5
♦ A 2
♣ A J 5

If you were West, playing 3NT, and, after North led ♣3, South played ♣J (and you win ♣K), you would find that you have been diddled out of a contract that would have succeeded if you had withheld ♣K. Play it out to see how it would go. You win ♣K and play diamonds, to drive out ♦A. South, after winning the first diamond, comes up with ♣A followed by ♣5.

Next time, look for less inspired opponents to play against!

That's a diversion and we must get back to basics. The hold-up technique is so productive on many hands, that there is a danger of misuse. It applies only when you do not have enough certain tricks to secure your contract, although, in the course of time, you may still employ it with a view to making overtricks. It is, therefore, generally right to hold up when you may have to lose the lead in order to establish extra tricks. But there are exceptions.

♠ A 7 2		♠ 10 6 5
♥ 8 7 5 2	N	♥ K
♦ K 6 3	W E	♦ A J 9 5 4
♣ A K J	S	♣ Q 8 3 2

West	North	East	South
1♥	pass	2♦	pass
2NT	pass	3NT	all pass

North leads ♠4, ♠5 from East, ♠Q from South.

Take the ♠A at once and, hoping that North holds the ♦Q, take the diamond finesse. If the suit divides 3-2 you have the tricks you need.

It would still be right to win the first trick if the ♠A had been in East's hand. Danger lurks. If you don't take the first trick, then South will. Seeing that isolated king, he will surely switch to hearts: a suit that will yield at least four tricks for the defence to go with that spade you failed to take.

Though irrelevant to this decision, note that South must have one of the king, queen or jack in spades because, if North held all three, he would lead the king.

To sum up:

- Use the hold-up when you must, or may have to, lose the lead at least once to make the contract UNLESS a likely switch to another suit would be more dangerous.

- If you decide to hold up your sure winner, the Rule of Seven helps you judge how many rounds you should hold up.

the hold-up with two 'stoppers'

The term 'stopper' is bridge slang but its meaning is not difficult to divine. It means that you hold a card which prevents the enemy from taking all the tricks in a particular suit immediately. We could have used the term previously when there was a stopper in the suit led which had to be held up to cut the enemy communications.

We will use it now to show that, even with two stoppers (which are most often, but not always, the ace and king) it can be right to hold up by refusing to win the first trick with either of them.

Hopefully, the reason for the hold-up technique with one stopper is understandable. When playing, you should have little difficulty in recognising when to employ it.

When you should hold up with two stoppers is difficult to work out logically and, for this reason, there is a formula that you can apply, with due discretion.

When you have to lose the lead twice to establish enough tricks to make the contract you should often hold off winning the first trick, even with two stoppers in the suit.

Here's where the mental difficulty lies:

	Q led	
A K 2		6 5 4

There may be the eventual danger that the defence will establish tricks in this suit but there looks to be no reason why you should not win the first trick and, when the suit is led again, hold up the second top winner to cut communications. We shall see that this is not good enough.

Let's put the holding into the context of a complete deal.

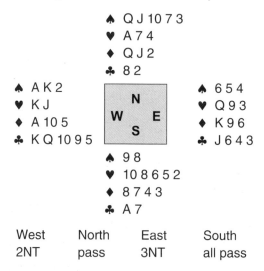

```
                    ♠ Q J 10 7 3
                    ♥ A 7 4
                    ♦ Q J 2
                    ♣ 8 2
  ♠ A K 2                             ♠ 6 5 4
  ♥ K J            ┌─────────┐        ♥ Q 9 3
  ♦ A 10 5         │    N    │        ♦ K 9 6
  ♣ K Q 10 9 5     │ W     E │        ♣ J 6 4 3
                   │    S    │
                   └─────────┘
                    ♠ 9 8
                    ♥ 10 8 6 5 2
                    ♦ 8 7 4 3
                    ♣ A 7
```

West	North	East	South
2NT	pass	3NT	all pass

North leads ♠Q.

West will count top winners (only four) and the extra tricks that can be established by driving out the ♣A (another four). One more must be established in hearts.

If West wins the opening lead and starts on clubs, South will win and play a second spade. West might play low on this but North will overtake his partner's card and lead another. North will retain his established spade winners along with the ♥A. The defence will make three spade tricks and two aces.

However, West is much better placed if he follows the formula and holds off winning the first trick. North will probably continue with another spade but now, when South wins the ♣A, he has no spade to return. The one heart trick can be established without danger since West still has that second stopper in spades.

By changing the hands slightly, we can make it more difficult to resist the temptation to win the first trick.

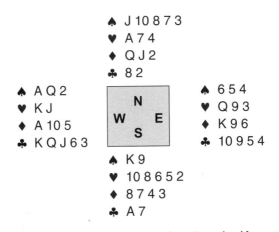

Against West's 3NT contract North leads ♠7 and ♠K appears from South. The ♠Q has become a certain top winner. West should play the two from ♠A K 2 and he should now do the same from ♠A Q 2.

While the hold-up was correct, the contract was not certain since North could have held both the missing aces.

When holding up, consider whether a switch by the defence to another suit would cause you greater problems.

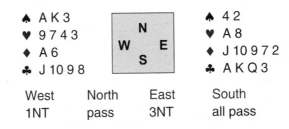

West	North	East	South
1NT	pass	3NT	all pass

North leads ♠6 and South plays ♠J.

With only eight top winners, the diamond suit needs to provide an extra trick and the probability is that the lead must be lost twice to establish it. The problem with holding up the first trick is that hearts are also vulnerable and you do not want a switch to that suit. It is best to win the initial lead, and start driving out ♦K and ♦Q.

quiz

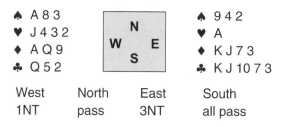

♠ A 8 3			♠ 9 4 2
♥ J 4 3 2			♥ A
♦ A Q 9			♦ K J 7 3
♣ Q 5 2			♣ K J 10 7 3

West	North	East	South
1NT	pass	3NT	all pass

North leads ♠Q, South playing ♠7. Should you duck ♠Q or should you win ♠A? Why?

Win your ♠A straightaway and play the ♣Q. You will then have one spade, one heart, four diamonds and four clubs. You must hope spades break 3-4 or that South started with ♠K 7 and failed to play ♠K on the first round – this is called 'blocking the suit'. If you duck, North might see the singleton ♥A in dummy and find the heart switch.

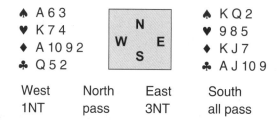

♠ A 6 3			♠ K Q 2
♥ K 7 4			♥ 9 8 5
♦ A 10 9 2			♦ K J 7
♣ Q 5 2			♣ A J 10 9

West	North	East	South
1NT	pass	3NT	all pass

The lead is ♥3; South wins ♥A and returns ♥6.

How do you play?

When South takes ♥A, your ♥K is the biggest heart and is like the ace. You can hold it up until the third round of hearts. Now when you take the club finesse, you do not mind if it loses, as South will have no more hearts left.

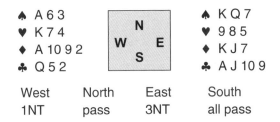

♠ A 6 3		♠ K Q 7
♥ K 7 4		♥ 9 8 5
♦ A 10 9 2		♦ K J 7
♣ Q 5 2		♣ A J 10 9

West	North	East	South
1NT	pass	3NT	all pass

North leads ♥3 and South plays ♥Q.

> This is not a position to duck. If you do South might return a heart through your ♥K 7 and you lose the first five heart tricks! Win and lead the ♣Q, playing low from dummy unless North plays the king. You make your contract if the club finesse works or if hearts break 4-3 so you only lose three heart tricks.

♠ Q J 10 9		♠ 8 7 2
♥ K 4 2		♥ A 9 3
♦ A Q 9		♦ K 7 4
♣ 9 5 2		♣ A K 10 7

West	North	East	South
1NT	pass	3NT	all pass

North leads ♥6, South plays ♥Q.

Should you duck the heart lead with two stops?

> You have two hearts, three diamonds and two clubs, so you need two spade tricks and will have to lose the lead twice to set them up. If North has ♥J 10 7 6 5 and South ♥Q 8, and the spade honours are split, you do not want South to win the first spade and return his last heart. It will knock out your second stopper and North will cash heart tricks when in with his high spade. Duck the heart and the contract should make.

15 recognising the danger hand

We looked at this deal to show the reason why the hold-up technique works.

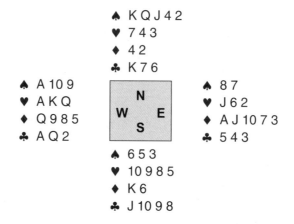

                    ♠ K Q J 4 2
                    ♥ 7 4 3
                    ♦ 4 2
                    ♣ K 7 6

    ♠ A 10 9   ♠ 8 7
    ♥ A K Q   N   ♥ J 6 2
    ♦ Q 9 8 5   W   E   ♦ A J 10 7 3
    ♣ A Q 2   S   ♣ 5 4 3

                    ♠ 6 5 3
                    ♥ 10 9 8 5
                    ♦ K 6
                    ♣ J 10 9 8

West is in 3NT and North leads ♠K. By refusing to win ♠A until the third round, declarer eliminates the threat of North's spade suit.

Declarer has cut communications between the defenders but he has also created a situation where he can safely lose the lead to South. No problem here since, by taking the diamond finesse, South is the only hand that can gain the lead in diamonds.

If there is a 'safe' hand, there must be a 'danger' hand. You won't need to be told that, in this example, it is North.

Here is another situation where one defender can threaten you if he gets the lead but the other defender is quite safe.

	4 led	
K J 10		7 6
	9 played	

North has surely led fourth highest from a long suit. If South had either the ace or queen, he would have played it. Therefore, you can place both those cards in the North hand. What would happen if South gained the lead? He would return partner's suit and, whether you played the king or the jack, North must win both the ace and queen and thereafter any small cards in the suit as well.

At best, you would have to cope with this layout:

	A Q 8 4	
K J 10		7 6
	9 5 3 2	

You win the first trick, but lose three more if South is on lead. Worse, it might be:

	A Q 8 4 3	
K J 10		7 6
	9 5 2	

Four tricks to be lost. Even worse:

	A Q 8 4 3 2	
K J 10		7 6
	9 5	

Therefore, South is the danger hand; the hand that you do not want to gain the lead. Conversely, North is the safe hand because after West wins the first trick with the jack, he still holds K 10 and North cannot lead the suit again without conceding a trick in it.

For the moment, we are not concerned about what you might do about this problem, just that you recognise it. The principle is often fundamental to the correct play of the hand, both in no trump and suit contracts.

We had a basic example earlier with an unprotected king.

K 2	5 4 3

If North leads this suit, K 2 will be a stopper. If South leads the suit the king will make a trick only if South holds the ace.

Suppose North has led another suit against West's no trump contract and tricks need to be established, but the lead can be lost only once. There is a 50% chance that North holds the ace, which means that, if South gains the lead, West's king will be dead.

What you do in this kind of situation is to assume the worst: that the ace is with North. South is the danger hand and, if you can prevent South from getting the lead, you will. Often, you will be powerless but recognising the problem from the outset makes you think a little harder and sometimes you may have an answer.

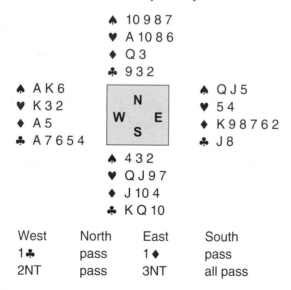

♠ 10 9 8 7
♥ A 10 8 6
♦ Q 3
♣ 9 3 2

♠ A K 6   ♠ Q J 5
♥ K 3 2   ♥ 5 4
♦ A 5   ♦ K 9 8 7 6 2
♣ A 7 6 5 4   ♣ J 8

♠ 4 3 2
♥ Q J 9 7
♦ J 10 4
♣ K Q 10

West	North	East	South
1♣	pass	1♦	pass
2NT	pass	3NT	all pass

North leads ♠10.

Declarer has to establish some diamond tricks. The odds, with eight cards between the two hands, are that the suit will break

3-2. So, after the opening lead is won by West (to keep a sure entry to the East hand), the ♦A is played followed by the ♦7 on which North plays the ♦Q.

This is a lucky development because North can be allowed to hold this trick. The safe hand is then on lead while the diamonds have become established (five tricks from the suit are enough) without letting the danger hand, South, gain the lead. Had declarer played ♦A, ♦K and another, you can see that South would win the third round and switch to ♥Q. One diamond and four heart tricks would defeat the contract.

Sometime in the future, you will be North and will frustrate declarer by playing ♦Q when West leads the ♦A!

to summarise

The danger hand is the one that you do not want to get the lead:

■ Because it holds winning tricks in a suit in which its partner has no more cards

■ Because a lead from the danger hand would be through a vulnerable holding.

Sometimes you must hope for the best. Sometimes you must fear the worst.

16 the danger hand: countermeasures

using the hold-up

A danger hand is not always evident at trick one; it may come up at any time during the play. Once you are aware of danger, there are sometimes countermeasures that can be taken. We saw that the hold-up is one and it needs to be looked at more closely in the context of identifying the danger hand.

Suppose North leads the seven and South plays the ten.

K Q 3	9 5 2

Before you automatically win with the queen, ask yourself if you should win this trick at all.

It all depends on recognising whether North or South is the danger hand.

It is probable that the lead is the fourth highest from a long suit. It is possible that it is from 7 4, hoping to find partner's suit. When in doubt, we suggested that you should assume that the lead is from a long suit and, therefore, the layout will be something like:

```
              A J 8 7 4
   K Q 3                   9 5 2
              10 6
```

If West wins the first trick, it will immediately make South the danger hand, since South's lead of the six gives North four tricks in the suit. If it is South who will gain the lead while tricks are established, this K Q 3 holding should be treated as the equivalent of A 3 2. In this example both together provide only one stopper in the suit. Therefore West should follow with a small card. South will play the six at trick two, North will win the ace and lead another. Now, South, having run out of cards in the suit, has become the safe hand.

However, if declarer knows that, when he loses the lead, it will be to the North hand, he should win the first trick since K 3 is still protection when that hand is on lead.

The difference is illustrated by these examples. In both cases West is in 3NT.

♠ K Q 3
♥ A K 2
♦ 9 8 7
♣ K 10 4 2

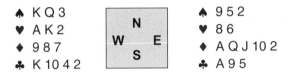

♠ 9 5 2
♥ 8 6
♦ A Q J 10 2
♣ A 9 5

North leads ♠7 and South plays ♠10.

West must play on diamonds to make the contract. That diamond king MAY be with South, so West should play small on the first trick. He gives up any hope of making two spade tricks, but he needs only one anyway.

Same contract, same lead.

♠ K Q 3
♥ A K 2
♦ A 9 8
♣ K J 10 2

♠ 9 5 2
♥ 8 6
♦ K J 10 4
♣ A 7 5 3

Here, South can be prevented from winning the lead until the contract is assured and West should win the first trick. After winning ♠Q, cross to East with ♣A and play ♦J, letting it run if South fails to produce ♦Q. If North wins ♦Q and returns a spade or a club, a ninth trick is immediately set up. Should North exit with a red suit, West, after cashing the established diamonds, simply takes the club finesse into the safe, North, hand.

There is no need to hold up on the first trick and it could be dangerous to do so. A switch to hearts by South would make life uncomfortable.

Here is a classic suit layout, much discussed in whist as well as bridge:

```
                    K Q 10 4 2
        A J 3                      6 5
                    9 8 7
```

North leads the king and West can work out that North holds a suit headed by K Q 10 because West can see the ace and jack. North would probably lead the fourth highest from a suit headed by just the K Q.

At one time, West would follow with the three and North would think that South had the ace or jack and lead the suit again, presenting West with a second trick in the suit. When it works, this hold-up manoeuvre is known as a 'Bath Coup' and West would be mighty pleased with himself. However, these days, the order in which South plays his cards should warn North against falling into the trap.

So, the question is whether West should win the first trick with the ace or hold up so that North is unable to lead the suit again without giving up an extra trick. Again, it depends …

It will usually, but not always, be correct to hold up since it buys time to establish tricks in the other suits.

It is vital to make a plan before playing a single card. It is very easy to make the obvious but fatally wrong play at trick one.

Declarer didn't stop and make a plan on this hand:

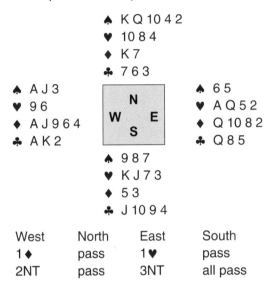

♠ K Q 10 4 2
♥ 10 8 4
♦ K 7
♣ 7 6 3

♠ A J 3
♥ 9 6
♦ A J 9 6 4
♣ A K 2

♠ 6 5
♥ A Q 5 2
♦ Q 10 8 2
♣ Q 8 5

♠ 9 8 7
♥ K J 7 3
♦ 5 3
♣ J 10 9 4

West	North	East	South
1♦	pass	1♥	pass
2NT	pass	3NT	all pass

North led ♠K and declarer, West, held up his ♠A. If North had
continued with the spades, declarer would have brought off a
Bath Coup and made two spade tricks. But North switched to ♥4
and this made life very difficult for declarer. Play it out for yourself
and see.

Declarer should have thought harder. He has six top tricks and
needs to find three more tricks to make the contract. He might
make one more spade, but only if North leads them. If North has
♥K he can make an extra trick by taking the finesse. Diamonds
are the best source of extra tricks – three more if North has ♦K or
four more if South has ♦K.

The main dangers are a heart switch by North and spades, but
only if South leads them.

South is the danger hand in spades and North is the danger hand
in hearts. Therefore, don't give North a chance to switch to hearts
until the diamonds are established.

Declarer should play his ♠A to win the first trick then cross to dummy with ♣Q and take the diamond finesse into the North hand. North will switch to hearts but the contract is safe.

If we change the hand slightly declarer has to withhold ♠A.

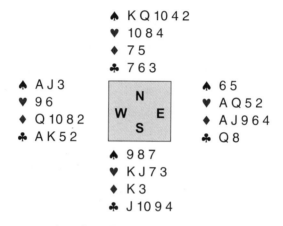

```
                    ♠ K Q 10 4 2
                    ♥ 10 8 4
                    ♦ 7 5
                    ♣ 7 6 3
  ♠ A J 3                              ♠ 6 5
  ♥ 9 6            N                   ♥ A Q 5 2
  ♦ Q 10 8 2   W      E                ♦ A J 9 6 4
  ♣ A K 5 2        S                   ♣ Q 8
                    ♠ 9 8 7
                    ♥ K J 7 3
                    ♦ K 3
                    ♣ J 10 9 4
```

Declarer now needs to buy time to establish the diamonds since the lead may have to be lost to South. Say North again switches to a heart at trick two. East's ♥A is played, ♣Q cashed, West's hand entered with a second club and, now, the diamond finesse is taken. It loses to South but the contract is safe. Both the spade and the heart (since South is on lead) suits are under control and nine tricks have been established.

the finesse and avoidance

We now want to look in more detail at ways to prevent the danger hand from gaining the lead.

The first involves making the best use of a position to which we gave particular attention earlier: the two-way finesse, see page 47. The suit distribution allowed you the choice of taking a finesse in either direction. For example:

You can choose whether to play for North or South to hold the queen. If four tricks are required from this suit you just have to make a guess. Having made your decision, you would start by leading the top card in the hand from which you intended to continue. For example, if you hope that South has the queen, you would first cash the king in case North held the queen singleton.

The choice could be dictated by the fact that one of the two defenders' hands is the danger hand. Here is a simple example:

	♠ A 9 7		♠ 4 2
	♥ K Q	N	♥ A 8 6
W	♦ A Q J 10 2	E	♦ 9 7 4
	♣ 9 6 3	S	♣ A Q J 10 2

West	North	East	South
1♦	pass	2♣	pass
2NT	pass	3NT	all pass

North leads ♠5.

Declarer may have to lose the lead and therefore employs the hold-up, winning his ♠A on the third round only.

North, with long spades to cash, is the danger hand. South should be out of spades: that was the point of holding up. There is a choice of finesses in diamonds and clubs, either of which will produce at least the three extra tricks to add to the six top winners. It is the club finesse that must be taken. If it loses, it will be to the safe (South) hand. ♥K and ♥Q should be played and then ♣9, playing ♣2 from dummy so the finesse can be repeated.

This is not so simple, but is equally logical:

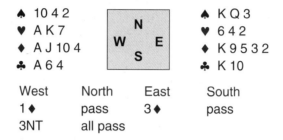

♠	10 4 2			♠	K Q 3
♥	A K 7		N	♥	6 4 2
♦	A J 10 4	W	E	♦	K 9 5 3 2
♣	A 6 4		S	♣	K 10

West	North	East	South
1♦	pass	3♦	pass
3NT	all pass		

North leads ♠7. The lead is ambiguous. It could be fourth highest or it could be top of a short suit. Let's assume you play East's ♠Q and South plays ♠9. This does not necessarily mean that North holds the ace but one thing is certain: losing the lead to South is perfectly safe.

So you should play a diamond to ♦A and follow with ♦J, letting it run if North fails to play ♦Q. South may win ♦Q, but the spades are still protected and you have nine tricks established.

If no danger hand existed, or you needed five tricks from the suit, it would be right to play off the two top diamonds since, with the extra chance that the queen may be singleton, the odds of making all five are better than the 50% finesse. Here, however, you have to guard against the hands being like this:

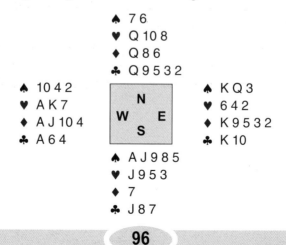

		♠	7 6		
		♥	Q 10 8		
		♦	Q 8 6		
		♣	Q 9 5 3 2		

♠	10 4 2			♠	K Q 3
♥	A K 7		N	♥	6 4 2
♦	A J 10 4	W	E	♦	K 9 5 3 2
♣	A 6 4		S	♣	K 10

		♠	A J 9 8 5		
		♥	J 9 5 3		
		♦	7		
		♣	J 8 7		

North made a short suit lead in the hope of finding his partner's best suit. South preserved his entry while playing the ♠9 to encourage (a high card from partner says that he likes the lead). Had the two top diamonds been cashed, North would inevitably win ♦Q and lead his second spade through East's ♠K 3.

It was not that North was definitely the danger hand but that South was certainly the safe hand that mattered.

Sometimes you will have to lose the lead twice to establish enough tricks and still have a danger hand to cope with.

♠ A K 2	N	♠ 4 3
♥ 6 2	W E	♥ A K 7 5 4
♦ Q J 10 2	S	♦ A 6 5 3
♣ K J 10 9		♣ Q 2

West	North	East	South
1NT	pass	3♥	pass
3NT	all pass		

North leads ♠Q.

Following the principle that it is correct, when no switch of suit can hurt, to hold up even with two stoppers, West lets ♠Q hold the first trick. North continues with ♠J.

There are opportunities for extra tricks in both diamonds and clubs. Which should you tackle first?

North threatens to set up his spade suit. He may have ♣A as an entry, but not in diamonds which can be finessed into the South hand. You need to get rid of North's possible entry first, so play a club.

This might be the complete deal:

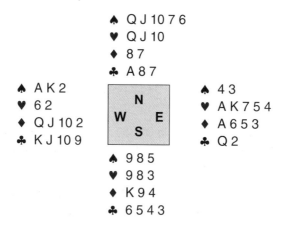

```
                    ♠ Q J 10 7 6
                    ♥ Q J 10
                    ♦ 8 7
                    ♣ A 8 7
  ♠ A K 2                          ♠ 4 3
  ♥ 6 2              N             ♥ A K 7 5 4
  ♦ Q J 10 2    W       E         ♦ A 6 5 3
  ♣ K J 10 9        S             ♣ Q 2
                    ♠ 9 8 5
                    ♥ 9 8 3
                    ♦ K 9 4
                    ♣ 6 5 4 3
```

If, after winning the second spade, West took the diamond finesse, South would lead his last spade to establish two tricks for North who would still have the ♣A as an entry.

Declarer must play clubs first and, after two tricks have been established in that suit, turn his attention to diamonds to establish two more by finessing into the safe hand.

The principle is this:

When you need tricks from two suits, and have two stoppers in the long suit led, you should first play the outside suit in which the danger hand has a possible entry.

The second possibility of preventing the danger hand gaining the lead merits a brief mention.

It is what is called 'avoidance play'. We had an example earlier.

A 3   K 9 8 7 6 2

Needing to establish tricks in this suit without allowing South to gain the lead, West played the ace and then the three. When North followed with the queen, he was allowed to hold the trick. It wasn't planned, but declarer took advantage of a fortunate development.

This, however, does need planning:

A K 5 4 2   7 6 3

You need to establish this suit for four tricks without allowing North to get the lead.

You could play off the two top winners and hope that South was the hand that held three cards in the suit. This will not work if North holds three cards.

If entries allow, lead twice from East. If South produces the queen on the second round, you let him hold that trick.

Note that if you cashed one top honour before leading towards the second, a good South could ditch the embarrassing queen on the first round.

Avoidance play is when you allow the safe hand to hold the trick, to prevent the danger hand getting the lead.

quiz

On each deal, identify the danger hand. Decide how to play the deal to keep the danger hand from gaining the lead.

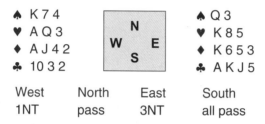

	♠ K 7 4			♠ Q 3
	♥ A Q 3			♥ K 8 5
	♦ A J 4 2			♦ K 6 5 3
	♣ 10 3 2			♣ A K J 5

West	North	East	South
1NT	pass	3NT	all pass

North leads ♠5. ♠Q loses to ♠A. South returns ♠10. You duck the second spade and North follows with ♠2, South plays ♠8, won by your ♠K.

> North is the danger hand with two winning spades to cash. You have one spade, three hearts, two diamonds and two clubs, eight top tricks, one more club will do. Play a club from hand to dummy's ♣J. Either it wins or, if it loses, ♣10 is now a winner.

	♠ A K 10			♠ 7 3
	♥ Q 3 2			♥ A K 8
	♦ A 10 6			♦ K J 5 3
	♣ 8 6 4 3			♣ K Q 7 2

West	North	East	South
1NT	pass	3NT	pass

North leads ♠4 to South's ♠Q.

> You have two spades, three hearts, two diamonds, seven top winners. It won't hurt if North gets in and leads another spade, your ♠10 will win the trick. So South is the danger hand, a spade lead through your ♠A 10 will set up all North's winners. Play ♥2 to ♥A and a diamond to ♦10. If it loses your ♦J is now a winner. When you get the lead back play a club towards ♣K Q to set up your ninth trick.

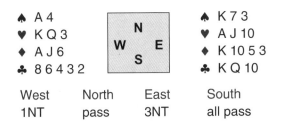

```
♠ A 4            N           ♠ K 7 3
♥ K Q 3      W     E         ♥ A J 10
♦ A J 6          S           ♦ K 10 5 3
♣ 8 6 4 3 2                  ♣ K Q 10
```

West	North	East	South
1NT	pass	3NT	all pass

North leads ♠5. South plays ♠Q.

You have two spades, three hearts, two diamonds, only seven top winners. Duck ♠Q and win the next spade. Play ♣2 to ♣K. If it wins play ♦3 to ♦J to set up a diamond trick. If the ♣K loses to ♣A, South plays another spade. Win ♠K. Play ♦3 to ♦A and ♦J, finessing if North plays low. If South wins and has another spade to play, the suit has broken 4-4. If it is 5-3, South will be out of spades and you have nine tricks.

```
♠ A J 8          N           ♠ 7 3
♥ Q 3 2      W     E         ♥ A K 7
♦ A 10 9         S           ♦ K J 8 7 2
♣ 8 6 4 3                    ♣ A K 7
```

West	North	East	South
		1♦	pass
2NT	pass	3NT	pass

North leads ♠4. South plays ♠Q.

You have one spade, three hearts, two diamonds and two clubs, one trick short. Win ♠A. South is the danger hand as a lead through your remaining ♠J 8 gives North all the spade tricks. Play ♥2 to ♥K and then lead a diamond to ♦10. If it wins you have nine tricks, more if the diamonds break 3-2 or you repeat the finesse. If it loses, dummy's diamonds are all winners. North is on lead and cannot continue spades without setting up your ♠J. If you try the finesse the other way, you risk South gaining the lead.

17 a trick from nowhere

Let's look again at a deal we had earlier:

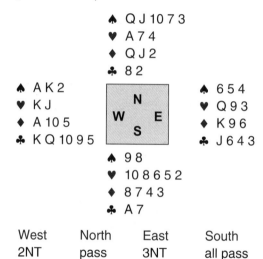

```
                    ♠ Q J 10 7 3
                    ♥ A 7 4
                    ♦ Q J 2
                    ♣ 8 2
   ♠ A K 2                          ♠ 6 5 4
   ♥ K J              N             ♥ Q 9 3
   ♦ A 10 5       W       E         ♦ K 9 6
   ♣ K Q 10 9 5      S              ♣ J 6 4 3
                    ♠ 9 8
                    ♥ 10 8 6 5 2
                    ♦ 8 7 4 3
                    ♣ A 7
```

West	North	East	South
2NT	pass	3NT	all pass

North leads ♠Q.

This deal was an example of the need to hold off winning the first trick with two stoppers in the suit led.

However, suppose, as West, you do decide to win the first trick and continue with the ♣K. South wins and leads the second spade. You decide to withhold your second top winner but North persists with the suit.

You now fear North holds the ♥A so, annoyed with yourself, you decide to make what you can and play off the winning clubs.

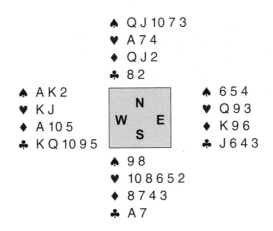

The cards that have been played are in red, leaving this layout, after declarer has won five tricks and the defence has won two tricks.

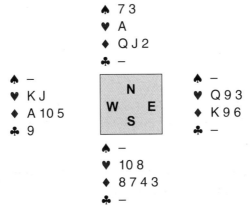

When West plays ♣9, can you see that North has a problem making a discard? The defence needs to make three more tricks to beat the contract and, in theory, North's ♠7 3 and ♥A will provide them. However, if he retains those three cards, he must discard a small diamond, allowing declarer to make three diamond tricks.

If he does discard ♦2, can declarer recognise the position? West leads ♦5 and ♦J appears from North and this means that if North started with ♦J 2 doubleton, South has ♦Q and it could be finessed. However, if North had only two diamonds, he must have a spare small heart, which he would choose to discard in preference to baring his diamond honour.

The alternative of a spade discard means giving up an established winner and discarding ♥A is unthinkable. North has the option only in respect of how he chooses to surrender.

Please don't think that you have to work out all of this. All you have done is run a long suit in the hope that something to your advantage will develop. In the critical position, instinct will probably direct the right play. North will probably agonise before making that no-win discard and you are perfectly entitled to draw a conclusion from his discomfort.

For the final hand in the main part of this book, we have that ultimate contract: West is in 7NT. As for the bidding? Let's just say that both East and West were feeling a bit frisky.

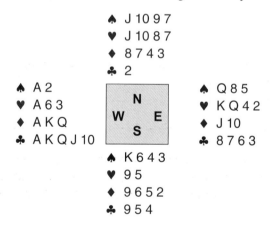

```
              ♠ J 10 9 7
              ♥ J 10 8 7
              ♦ 8 7 4 3
              ♣ 2
  ♠ A 2              ┌─────────┐    ♠ Q 8 5
  ♥ A 6 3            │    N    │    ♥ K Q 4 2
  ♦ A K Q         W  │         │ E  ♦ J 10
  ♣ A K Q J 10       │    S    │    ♣ 8 7 6 3
                     └─────────┘
              ♠ K 6 4 3
              ♥ 9 5
              ♦ 9 6 5 2
              ♣ 9 5 4
```

North leads ♠J.

Declarer played East's ♠Q on ♠J lead, South covered with ♠K and West had to win ♠A.

Give the play a go before reading on.

Unfortunately, there were only twelve top tricks. Basically, West had to hope that the hearts divided 3-3, which appeared to be the only chance for the thirteenth trick. As you can see from the diagram, this was not destined to happen.

There was, however, no need to play hearts immediately. West cashed all his winners in clubs and diamonds and when the last winner, ♦Q, was about to be played, this was the position:

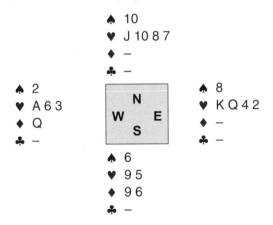

When ♦Q was led, what could North discard? If ♠10, East's ♠8 would be a winner. If ♥7, then ♠8 is thrown from East and four heart tricks materialise.

The purpose of these two examples is to give a final tip:

When there seems to be no legitimate play for the contract, run a long suit and other top winners. The defenders may be in trouble with their discards and that extra trick may come from nowhere.

Putting one or both players in a position where whatever they throw away is to declarer's advantage is called a squeeze.

18 how to plan the play

When dummy goes down there is a lot to think about. You must STOP and make a cunning plan of how you are going to achieve your contract. This plan will only come into being by careful, logical thought on your part. It is no easy task to think your way through 13 tricks and most of us find it helpful to have a structure on which we can hang our thinking. One way is to become a SWOT. This stands for:

Strengths
: first, count your top winners, which are those tricks that you can make without losing the lead.

Weakness
: second, work out how many tricks you are short of your target.

Opportunities
: third, inspect each suit in turn looking for chances to make extra tricks.

Threats
: fourth, think about what can go wrong with your plan and how you can counter it.

Even if it seems obvious which card you are going to play at trick one STOP AND THINK. Do not touch a card until you have a plan. At that moment you can see 27 cards – your own hand, dummy and the opening lead – so it is the best time to do your planning. It is all too easy to dive straight in only to realise later that you made a fatal error at trick one.

Discipline yourself to think first, play later.

hands to play and practise

The primary objective in learning bridge is to get four people round a table playing the game and enjoying the stimulating challenge that it presents – the sooner the better. The 24 hands that follow are based on the techniques explained in the book. While they can be studied from the text, it will be more instructive, and much greater fun, if you have two or three friends who can play them with you. Since one person is always dummy, you can play perfectly satisfactorily with three players by leaving the East chair vacant.

Prepare the hands in advance from the complete deal given with the answers. Sort the pack into suits and distribute the suit as shown. Store the complete deal in four envelopes marked W, N, S or E with the hand number on it. Note North's opening lead and any other instructions.

Six deals will normally be enough to play in one session since you will want to allow time for discussion and analysis. If the participants have access to this book, all could prepare and bring two deals but everybody will need to have two packs of cards. The person who prepared a particular deal should not be the declarer when it is played. Make that player East, with four players, or a defender, with three. Rotate the positions so that everyone gets a go at being declarer (West).

Play the cards 'duplicate style'. Each player puts the card down directly in front of himself. When the four cards to a trick have been played, each card is turned face down, upright when a player's side has won that trick and lengthways when it has been lost.

Here, for example, West (the declarer) has won the first three tricks but lost the fourth.

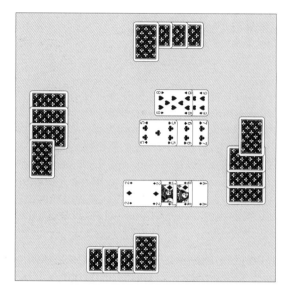

After the play has finished, you count the number of cards pointing in your direction to work out the number of tricks won by your side. Each player's original hand has been retained and this enables the deal to be revised with all four hands visible. You can even play the hand through again with a different declarer to check that the lesson is understood.

The first twelve hands are intended to be easier than the next twelve. On all of them it is far more important to understand how the contract should be played than it is to get it right first time. Bridge is primarily for fun. Its attraction is the intellectual challenge that it offers and the satisfaction gained, at all levels of ability, in logically working out the right line of play. In this respect, much comes with practice and experience.

In all the problems you are declarer (West) and your task is to plan the play.

hands to play

1

	♠ A K 8			♠ Q 7 3
	♥ A 8 7			♥ K 10 5
	♦ 8 6 5			♦ A 7 4 3 2
	♣ A K 4 2			♣ 8 6

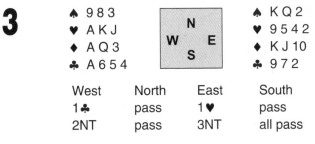

West	North	East	South
1♣	pass	1♦	pass
2NT	pass	3NT	all pass

North leads ♠J.

2

	♠ A Q			♠ K 7 4 2
	♥ K Q 3			♥ 8 7 2
	♦ A 10 6 3			♦ 9 8 5 2
	♣ A K 8 2			♣ Q J

West	North	East	South
2NT	pass	3♣	pass
3♦	pass	3NT	all pass

East's 3♣ bid is Stayman. West's 3♦ reply denies a 4-card major suit and East bids 3NT.

North leads ♥5 and South follows with ♥J.

3

	♠ 9 8 3			♠ K Q 2
	♥ A K J			♥ 9 5 4 2
	♦ A Q 3			♦ K J 10
	♣ A 6 5 4			♣ 9 7 2

West	North	East	South
1♣	pass	1♥	pass
2NT	pass	3NT	all pass

North leads ♥7.

1

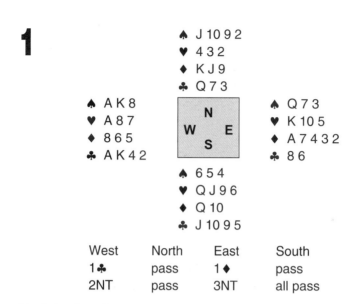

♠ J 10 9 2
♥ 4 3 2
♦ K J 9
♣ Q 7 3

♠ A K 8
♥ A 8 7
♦ 8 6 5
♣ A K 4 2

♠ Q 7 3
♥ K 10 5
♦ A 7 4 3 2
♣ 8 6

♠ 6 5 4
♥ Q J 9 6
♦ Q 10
♣ J 10 9 5

West	North	East	South
1♣	pass	1♦	pass
2NT	pass	3NT	all pass

North leads ♠J.

Strengths	There are eight top winners.
Weakness	One trick.
Opportunities	Declarer has eight diamonds and so extra tricks can be established by driving out the defenders' high cards. See Chapter 5.
Threats	If the defenders' diamonds split 5-0 no extra tricks can be made. This is not very likely.
Plan	After winning the first trick in the West hand, declarer should play a small diamond from both hands. When the lead is regained, a small diamond from both hands is again played.

Declarer cannot be prevented from winning the lead back again and now ♦A draws the last diamond from the defenders and East's final two small cards in the suit both win tricks. Ten tricks should be made on this line of play.

2

	♠ 10 5 3	
	♥ A 10 6 5 4	
	♦ K 7	
	♣ 10 7 4	

♠ A Q		♠ K 7 4 2
♥ K Q 3	N	♥ 8 7 2
♦ A 10 6 3	W E	♦ 9 8 5 2
♣ A K 8 2	S	♣ Q J

	♠ J 9 8 6	
	♥ J 9	
	♦ Q J 4	
	♣ 9 6 5 3	

West	North	East	South
2NT	pass	3♣	pass
3♦	pass	3NT	all pass

North leads ♥5 and South plays ♥J.

Strengths	Nine top tricks after the opening lead.
Weakness	None
Opportunities	
Threats	Care must be taken in the order in which the top tricks are cashed to avoid any blockage. See Chapter 3.
Plan	Cash both ♠A and ♠Q. Cross to dummy by leading a low club and cash ♠K and East's other club winner. Return to West with ♦A to cash ♣A and ♣K.

3

```
              ♠ A 7 4
              ♥ Q 10 8 7 3
              ♦ 8 6 2
              ♣ Q 8
♠ 9 8 3                        ♠ K Q 2
♥ A K J          N            ♥ 9 5 4 2
♦ A K J      W     E          ♦ Q 10 3
♣ A 6 5 4        S            ♣ 9 7 2
              ♠ J 10 6 5
              ♥ 6
              ♦ 9 7 5 4
              ♣ K J 10 3
```

West	North	East	South
2NT	pass	3NT	all pass

North leads the ♥7.

Strengths	The lead makes ♥J into a winner. With it, the tally of top winners comes to seven.
Weakness	Two more tricks to be found.
Opportunities	One more trick can certainly be established from East's K Q 2 in spades. However, as you can see from the diagram, two tricks can come from the spade suit since North holds the ♠A. This is an example of a finesse. See Chapter 9. The 50% chance that North holds the ♠A is better than playing to establish a small card in clubs, which needs a 3-3 break and is only a 36% chance.
Threats	If South has ♠A declarer will still be a trick short and will have to hope the hearts or clubs break 3-3. A kind break in hearts is not likely after the lead.
Plan	Lead towards East's K Q 2. It is unlikely that North would play the ace first time, so East's queen takes the trick. A second lead from West towards K 2 produces the second trick in the suit.

hands to play

4

♠ 4 3 2
♥ A K Q J
♦ Q 2
♣ A 4 3 2

	N	
W		E
	S	

♠ A K Q 5
♥ 7 6
♦ J 5 3
♣ J 10 9 5

West	North	East	South
1♥	pass	1♠	pass
1NT	pass	3NT	all pass

North leads ♠J.

5

♠ A 7
♥ A 6 5 2
♦ A 10 5
♣ J 8 7 5

	N	
W		E
	S	

♠ K 8 6 4 2
♥ 9
♦ K J 3 2
♣ K Q 10

West	North	East	South
1NT	pass	3♠	pass
3NT	all pass		

North leads ♥K.

6

♠ A 4
♥ A 6 4 2
♦ 7 4
♣ A K 7 4 3

	N	
W		E
	S	

♠ J 8 7 6 2
♥ K
♦ A K Q 6 5
♣ 10 8

West	North	East	South
1♣	pass	1♠	pass
1NT	pass	3♦	pass
3NT	all pass		

North leads ♥Q.

4

```
          ♠ J 10 9 8
          ♥ 4 3 2
          ♦ A 10 4
          ♣ K Q 6
♠ 4 3 2              ♠ A K Q 5
♥ A K Q J    N       ♥ 7 6
♦ Q 2     W     E    ♦ J 5 3
♣ A 4 3 2    S       ♣ J 10 9 5
          ♠ 7 6
          ♥ 10 9 8 5
          ♦ K 9 8 7 6
          ♣ 8 7
```

West	North	East	South
1♥	pass	1♠	pass
1NT	pass	3NT	all pass

North leads ♠J.

Strengths	Eight top winners – seven in spades and hearts plus ♣A.
Weakness	One more trick needed.
Opportunities	A second club trick or one diamond trick. Note East-West's diamond holding. If either defender leads this suit, declarer will be able to make his ninth trick in it. West therefore has no fear about losing the lead and has plenty of time to establish one extra trick in clubs from East's J 10 9 by driving out ♣Q and ♣K. See Chapter 8.
Threats	None. West can see that the contract is certain to make on any distribution.
Plan	East's ♣J is played at trick two and left to ride, to be won by North. The finesse in the suit can be repeated and two extra tricks would be made in clubs if the defenders held one honour each, giving declarer an overtrick. Not here – but the contract is secure.

5

		♠ 5 3	
		♥ K Q J 10 4	
		♦ Q 7	
		♣ 9 6 3 2	

♠ A 7			♠ K 8 6 4 2
♥ A 6 5 2	**N**		♥ 9
♦ A 10 5	**W E**		♦ K J 3 2
♣ J 8 7 5	**S**		♣ K Q 10

		♠ Q J 10 9	
		♥ 8 7 3	
		♦ 9 8 6 4	
		♣ A 4	

West	North	East	South
1NT	pass	3♠	pass
3NT	all pass		

North leads ♥K.

Strengths	Five top tricks.
Weakness	Four more tricks needed.
Opportunities	A successful diamond finesse will produce one more trick. See Chapter 9. Clubs will yield three more tricks once the ace has been driven out. See Chapter 4.
Threats	Hearts are the danger here as declarer has only the ace and four small cards. The lead means the defence have found their source of tricks. The way to counter this is to hold up ♥A until the third round so that if South gets the lead he has no hearts to lead back. See Chapter 14. Then play to keep North off lead, hoping he does not have ♣A.
Plan	Hope North has ♦Q and South has ♣A. Hold up the ♥A until the third round. Play clubs. Finesse diamonds so that if the finesse were to fail it would be South who gains the lead. South is the safe hand. See Chapter 15.

6

```
             ♠ K 3
             ♥ Q J 10 7 3
             ♦ 8 2
             ♣ J 9 5 2
♠ A 4                        ♠ J 8 7 6 2
♥ A 6 4 2       N            ♥ K
♦ 7 4       W     E          ♦ A K Q 6 5
♣ A K 7 4 3     S            ♣ 10 8
             ♠ Q 10 9 5
             ♥ 9 8 5
             ♦ J 10 9 3
             ♣ Q 6
```

West	North	East	South
1♣	pass	1♠	pass
1NT	pass	3♦	pass
3NT	all pass		

North leads ♥Q.

Strengths	Eight top winners.
Weakness	One more trick needed.
Opportunities	If the diamonds break 3-3 there are two extra tricks and if they break 4-2 there is the needed extra trick. There is also the chance to make extra tricks in clubs.
Threats	Six cards are most likely to break 4-2 – a 48% chance, so declarer can win three tricks, lose one and take the last diamond trick. To do this he has to be able to enter dummy in another suit and the opening lead has taken away his only entry outside the diamond suit. Therefore he must give up his diamond loser straight away and secure his contract rather than rely on the 35% chance of the diamonds breaking 3-3. See Chapter 6.
Plan	Play a small diamond from both hands at trick two.

hands to play

7

♠ A 7 4
♥ K 10
♦ K 8 7
♣ Q J 10 9 8

	N	
W		E
	S	

♠ K 5 2
♥ A Q J
♦ A 4 3 2
♣ 6 5 3

West	North	East	South
1NT	pass	3NT	all pass

North leads ♠Q.

8

♠ 10 6 4
♥ A K 2
♦ A 10 9 6 4
♣ J 2

	N	
W		E
	S	

♠ A K 3 2
♥ 7 5 4 3
♦ Q J 3
♣ Q 3

West	North	East	South
1NT	pass	2♣	pass
2♦	pass	2NT	all pass

East's 2♣ bid is the Stayman convention, looking to play in spades or hearts, in preference to no trumps, if West has four cards in either suit. West's 2♦ denies a 4-card major.

North leads ♠8.

9

♠ A K
♥ A Q 10
♦ K Q 4 2
♣ A 9 8 2

	N	
W		E
	S	

♠ 8 7 6
♥ 7 6 3
♦ 9 8
♣ K Q 6 4 3

West	North	East	South
2NT	pass	3NT	all pass

North leads ♠Q.

7

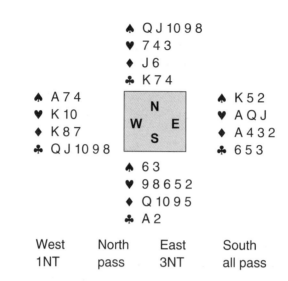

♠ Q J 10 9 8
♥ 7 4 3
♦ J 6
♣ K 7 4

♠ A 7 4
♥ K 10
♦ K 8 7
♣ Q J 10 9 8

N W E S

♠ K 5 2
♥ A Q J
♦ A 4 3 2
♣ 6 5 3

♠ 6 3
♥ 9 8 6 5 2
♦ Q 10 9 5
♣ A 2

West	North	East	South
1NT	pass	3NT	all pass

North leads ♠Q.

Strengths	Seven top winners.
Weakness	Two more tricks needed.
Opportunities	Two more from the club suit. See Chapter 4.
Threats	The lead has to be given up twice. In such cases it is correct to hold off winning the first spade even though there are two top winners in the suit. No switch of suit at trick two will damage declarer. See what would happen if declarer won the first spade, in either hand. South would win ♣A and play his second spade, establishing three spade tricks for North who will gain the lead with ♣K. See Chapter 14.
Plan	North will probably play a second spade and West should start establishing club tricks. Provided that ♣A and ♣K are not both in North's hand, three clubs will be established giving declarer an overtrick.

8

	♠ 8 7	
	♥ Q 10 9	
	♦ K 8 7 2	
	♣ K 10 8 6	

♠ 10 6 4		♠ A K 3 2
♥ A K 2	**N**	♥ 7 5 4 3
♦ A 10 9 6 4	**W E**	♦ Q J 3
♣ J 2	**S**	♣ Q 3

	♠ Q J 9 5	
	♥ J 8 6	
	♦ 5	
	♣ A 9 7 5 4	

West	North	East	South
1NT	pass	2♣	pass
2♦	pass	2NT	all pass

North leads the ♠8.

Strengths	Five top tricks.
Weakness	Four more tricks needed.
Opportunities	Diamonds will yield three or four extra tricks, depending on who has ♦K. See Chapter 9. Spades and hearts both have the potential for an extra trick with a 3-3 break – less likely than 4-2 but not improbable.
Threats	The Rule of Eleven (11 – 8 = 3) (see Chapter 12) might lead declarer to calculate that West's ♠10 will take the first trick. If the lead were fourth highest, it would be from Q J 9 8 and the queen would normally be chosen. See Chapter 11. A switch to clubs will beat the contract provided the defenders play the suit to best advantage.
Plan	West should win the first trick in East and lead the ♦Q intending to finesse. As it happens, the finesse loses but North, who has chosen to lead passively at trick one, may do so again at trick three.

9

```
              ♠ Q J 9 4 3
              ♥ K J 4 2
              ♦ A 10 3
              ♣ 7
♠ A K                          ♠ 8 7 6
♥ A Q 10        N              ♥ 7 6 3
♦ K Q 4 2     W   E            ♦ 9 8
♣ A 9 8 2       S              ♣ K Q 6 4 3
              ♠ 10 5 2
              ♥ 9 8 5
              ♦ J 7 6 5
              ♣ J 10 5
```

West	North	East	South
2NT	pass	3NT	all pass

North leads ♠Q.

Strengths	Six top tricks.
Weakness	Three more tricks needed.
Opportunities	Two extra tricks from clubs providing they break 2-2 or 3-1. One or two tricks from diamonds, depending on the position of ♦A.
Threats	At first sight, there appear to be no problems. When all appears easy, look for the hidden danger. After winning the first trick, West might lead ♣2 to dummy's king. If so, he has blocked the suit. He is unable to take five tricks in it.
Plan	West must preserve ♣2 to keep communications open. One way is to start with ♣A, then ♣8 to ♣Q and play ♣9 on East's ♣K. See Chapter 7.

hands to play

10

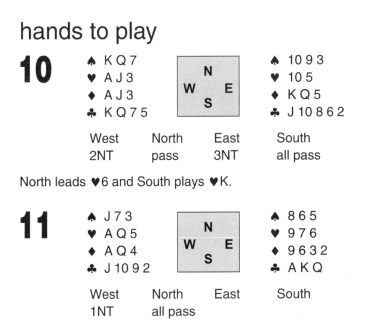

♠ K Q 7
♥ A J 3
♦ A J 3
♣ K Q 7 5

♠ 10 9 3
♥ 10 5
♦ K Q 5
♣ J 10 8 6 2

West	North	East	South
2NT	pass	3NT	all pass

North leads ♥6 and South plays ♥K.

11

♠ J 7 3
♥ A Q 5
♦ A Q 4
♣ J 10 9 2

♠ 8 6 5
♥ 9 7 6
♦ 9 6 3 2
♣ A K Q

West	North	East	South
1NT	all pass		

North leads the ♠4; South follows with the ♠Q and returns the
♠ 9. North wins the next four tricks in spades with the A K 10 2
and then plays the ♣6.

12

♠ A K 8 2
♥ 9 5 2
♦ K 10 3
♣ A 6 5

♠ 6 3
♥ A Q 10 6
♦ Q 9 4 2
♣ K 9 8

West	North	East	South
1NT	pass	2♣	pass
2♠	pass	2NT	pass
3NT	all pass		

West's 2♠ response shows, for East's purposes, four cards in the
wrong major suit.

North leads ♥7.

10

	♠ A 4	
	♥ Q 9 8 6 2	
	♦ 7 6 4 2	
	♣ 9 3	

♠ K Q 7		♠ 10 9 3
♥ A J 3	**N**	♥ 10 5
♦ A J 3	**W E**	♦ K Q 5
♣ K Q 7 5	**S**	♣ J 10 8 6 2

	♠ J 8 6 5 2	
	♥ K 7 4	
	♦ 10 9 8	
	♣ A 4	

West	North	East	South
2NT	pass	3NT	all pass

North leads ♥6.

Strengths	Four top tricks.
Weakness	Five more tricks needed.
Opportunities	Clubs and spades both have the potential to make extra tricks.
Threats	After the initial lead, the combination of ♥A J 3 in West's hand and ♥10 5 in East's makes for two sure stoppers in the suit. East's ♥5 must be played at trick one and West must win, not hold up, when South plays ♥K. West's ♥J 3 and East's ♥10 ensures a second trick in the suit with only ♥Q outstanding. Either playing East's ♥10 or holding off winning the first trick will put the contract in jeopardy.
Plan	After winning the first trick, West drives out ♣A and should come to nine tricks without difficulty. No doubt South will play another heart, after winning ♣A, establishing the ninth trick for declarer. He should take them before trying for an overtrick in spades.

11

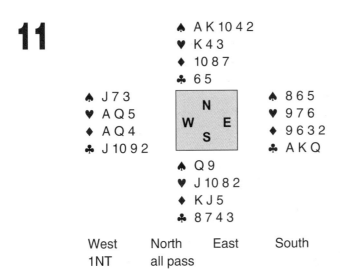

♠ A K 10 4 2
♥ K 4 3
♦ 10 8 7
♣ 6 5

♠ J 7 3
♥ A Q 5
♦ A Q 4
♣ J 10 9 2

N W E S

♠ 8 6 5
♥ 9 7 6
♦ 9 6 3 2
♣ A K Q

♠ Q 9
♥ J 10 8 2
♦ K J 5
♣ 8 7 4 3

West	North	East	South
1NT	all pass		

North leads the ♠4, South plays the ♠Q and returns the ♠9. North wins the next four tricks in the suit with ♠A K 10 2 and then plays the ♣6.

Strengths	Six top tricks.
Weakness	One more trick needed.
Opportunities	Both red suits offer the chance to make an extra trick. You only need one finesse to work. See Chapter 10. But which suit to choose?
Threats	Declarer needs to be able to enter the East hand to try the other finesse if the first choice fails. The only entries are in clubs so he must not play off the top three clubs first. See Chapter 7.
Plan	Say the heart finesse is tried first but ♥Q loses to ♥K. Enter dummy with a club, cash the third top club and take the diamond finesse. Provided that South has one of the red kings, the contract makes. If the first finesse succeeds, try the second one before cashing the ace of that suit. There is no danger and an overtrick results if South has both kings.

12

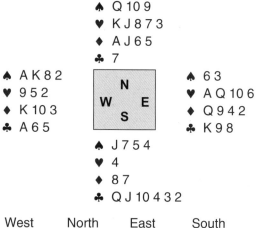

	♠ Q 10 9	
	♥ K J 8 7 3	
	♦ A J 6 5	
	♣ 7	
♠ A K 8 2		♠ 6 3
♥ 9 5 2		♥ A Q 10 6
♦ K 10 3		♦ Q 9 4 2
♣ A 6 5		♣ K 9 8
	♠ J 7 5 4	
	♥ 4	
	♦ 8 7	
	♣ Q J 10 4 3 2	

West	North	East	South
1NT	pass	2♣	pass
2♠	pass	2NT	pass
3NT	all pass		

North leads the ♥7.

Strengths	Five top tricks.
Weakness	Four more tricks needed.
Opportunities	Hearts and a diamond. West should apply the Rule of Eleven (11 − 7 = 4) and realise that ♥9 will win the first trick if the lead is fourth highest. See Chapter 12.
Threats	Playing any of East's top three cards at trick one costs a trick. Work out how.
Plan	East's ♥6 is played and, sure enough, West can win cheaply. He can now play ♥2 towards East covering whatever card North plays with the cheapest card in dummy. He returns to hand with a spade and repeats the heart finesse. With four heart tricks and four top winners, the ninth can come from diamonds before cashing the remaining black suit winners.

hands to play

13

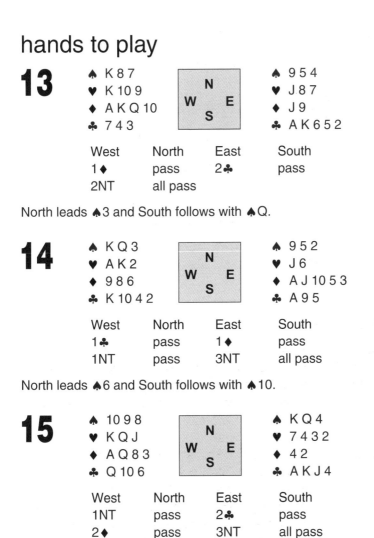

♠ K 8 7
♥ K 10 9
♦ A K Q 10
♣ 7 4 3

♠ 9 5 4
♥ J 8 7
♦ J 9
♣ A K 6 5 2

West	North	East	South
1♦	pass	2♣	pass
2NT	all pass		

North leads ♠3 and South follows with ♠Q.

14

♠ K Q 3
♥ A K 2
♦ 9 8 6
♣ K 10 4 2

♠ 9 5 2
♥ J 6
♦ A J 10 5 3
♣ A 9 5

West	North	East	South
1♣	pass	1♦	pass
1NT	pass	3NT	all pass

North leads ♠6 and South follows with ♠10.

15

♠ 10 9 8
♥ K Q J
♦ A Q 8 3
♣ Q 10 6

♠ K Q 4
♥ 7 4 3 2
♦ 4 2
♣ A K J 4

West	North	East	South
1NT	pass	2♣	pass
2♦	pass	3NT	all pass

North leads ♦J and South follows with ♦K.

13

♠ A J 6 3 2
♥ A 6 5
♦ 7 4
♣ 10 9 8

♠ K 8 7　　　　　　　　　　♠ 9 5 4
♥ K 10 9　　　　 N　　　　♥ J 8 7
♦ A K Q 10　 W　 E　　♦ J 9
♣ 7 4 3　　　　　 S　　　　♣ A K 6 5 2

♠ Q 10
♥ Q 4 3 2
♦ 8 6 5 3 2
♣ Q J

West	North	East	South
1♦	pass	2♣	pass
2NT	all pass		

North leads ♠3.

Strengths	Six top tricks.
Weakness	Two more tricks needed.
Opportunities	West must win the ♠K now or he never will. Clubs are a potential source of the vital extra trick. Hearts are another possibility.
Threats	West cannot afford to look to clubs for the extra trick. It would mean giving up a trick and, now, North will take four spade tricks and there is still ♥A in enemy hands. An alternative must be sought and a successful heart finesse is the answer. However West has to guess whether to play for South to hold ♥A or ♥Q.
Plan	Play ♥J from East since South may be tempted to cover with ♥Q. If South plays low, assume that he does not hold the queen and play West's king. Tough luck if, as here, South has the queen but refuses to cover ♥J. That would be excellent defence.

14

```
              ♠ A J 8 6 4
              ♥ 10 7 3
              ♦ Q 4 2
              ♣ 7 3
♠ K Q 3                          ♠ 9 5 2
♥ A K 2         N                ♥ J 6
♦ 9 8 6       W   E              ♦ A J 10 5 3
♣ K 10 4 2      S                ♣ A 9 5
              ♠ 10 7
              ♥ Q 9 8 5 4
              ♦ K 7
              ♣ Q J 8 6
```

West	North	East	South
1♣	pass	1♦	pass
1NT	pass	3NT	all pass

North leads ♠6.

Strengths	There are five top winners.
Weakness	Four more tricks needed.
Opportunities	One certain spade trick and a second if South holds ♠A. The diamonds can provide the extra three tricks with a double finesse, provided ♦K and ♦Q are in different hands or North has both of them. See Chapter 9.
Threats	On the first trick, South plays the ♠10 and West must not win. If he does, South will be able to lead another spade through ♠K when South gains the lead with a diamond. It is not only possible but probable South will gain the lead.
Plan	Treat ♠K Q 3 as if it were ♠A 3 2 and hold up. Win the third spade and take the double diamond finesse. When South gains the lead with ♦K, he has no spade to return.

15

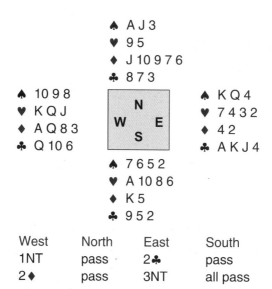

♠ A J 3
♥ 9 5
♦ J 10 9 7 6
♣ 8 7 3

♠ 10 9 8
♥ K Q J
♦ A Q 8 3
♣ Q 10 6

♠ K Q 4
♥ 7 4 3 2
♦ 4 2
♣ A K J 4

♠ 7 6 5 2
♥ A 10 8 6
♦ K 5
♣ 9 5 2

West	North	East	South
1NT	pass	2♣	pass
2♦	pass	3NT	all pass

North leads ♦J and South plays ♦K on this lead. The lead looks highly satisfactory from West's point of view; here's a finesse that he doesn't need to take.

Strengths	Six top winners: two in diamonds after the lead, and four in clubs.
Weakness	Three more tricks needed.
Opportunities	Two tricks in hearts and one or two spades.
Threats	The lead has to be lost twice to set up hearts and spades and West must follow basic technique of holding up, even with two winners. See Chapter 14. See what happens if West wins ♦A. He plays ♥K and South wins to fire back a diamond and soon West's ♦Q is gone. North has three diamond winners and will get in with ♠A.
Plan	West must hold off winning the first trick! He can win the second round of diamonds and lead the ♥K. But, now, South does not have a diamond to lead and West has time to establish a spade trick.

hands to play

16

♠ A 10 6		♠ Q
♥ A J 7 2		♥ K 4 3
♦ A 4 2	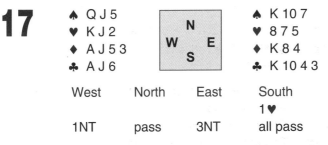	♦ Q J 7 5
♣ K 10 3		♣ A J 9 4 2

West	North	East	South
1♥	pass	2♣	pass
2NT	pass	3♥	pass
3NT	all pass		

East's 3♥ (showing three hearts) was forcing to game.

North leads ♠3 and East's ♠Q is covered by South's ♠K.

17

♠ Q J 5		♠ K 10 7
♥ K J 2		♥ 8 7 5
♦ A J 5 3		♦ K 8 4
♣ A J 6		♣ K 10 4 3

West	North	East	South
			1♥
1NT	pass	3NT	all pass

North leads ♥Q. South wins with ♥A and returns ♥10.

18

♠ A 7 3		♠ Q 4
♥ 7 6 2		♥ A K Q
♦ A K 3 2		♦ Q 10 5 4
♣ K 3 2		♣ 7 6 5 4

West	North	East	South
1NT	pass	3NT	all pass

North leads ♣Q and South wins ♣A and returns ♣9.

16

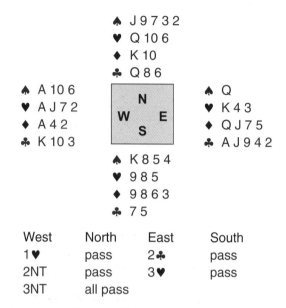

	♠ J 9 7 3 2	
	♥ Q 10 6	
	♦ K 10	
	♣ Q 8 6	

♠ A 10 6		♠ Q
♥ A J 7 2	**N**	♥ K 4 3
♦ A 4 2	**W E**	♦ Q J 7 5
♣ K 10 3	**S**	♣ A J 9 4 2

	♠ K 8 5 4	
	♥ 9 8 5	
	♦ 9 8 6 3	
	♣ 7 5	

West	North	East	South
1♥	pass	2♣	pass
2NT	pass	3♥	pass
3NT	all pass		

North leads ♠3 and East's ♠Q is covered by South's ♠K.

Strengths	Five top tricks.
Weakness	Four more tricks needed.
Opportunities	All the suits can yield extra tricks.
Threats	West can identify North's lead as fourth highest (see Chapter 12) and ♠3 shows that the suit must divide 5-4. Holding up the ♠A will not cut communications (see Chapter 14) but, after winning the first trick, West's ♠10 6 means that the defenders are unable to take their spade tricks immediately, provided South, the danger hand, does not get the lead. See Chapter 15.
Plan	Win with ♠A. Take ♣A, in case ♣Q is singleton, then play low towards ♣K 10. The finesse loses but sets up three club tricks. If North continues spades, there's the ninth trick. If he sensibly leads a club, take the diamond finesse by running ♦Q, also into the safe North hand.

17

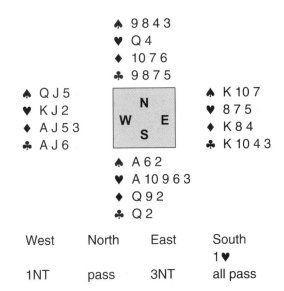

```
              ♠ 9 8 4 3
              ♥ Q 4
              ♦ 10 7 6
              ♣ 9 8 7 5
♠ Q J 5                          ♠ K 10 7
♥ K J 2          N               ♥ 8 7 5
♦ A J 5 3    W       E           ♦ K 8 4
♣ A J 6          S               ♣ K 10 4 3
              ♠ A 6 2
              ♥ A 10 9 6 3
              ♦ Q 9 2
              ♣ Q 2
```

West	North	East	South
			1♥
1NT	pass	3NT	all pass

North leads ♥Q. South wins with ♥A and returns ♥10.

Strengths	Four top tricks.
Weakness	Five more tricks needed.
Opportunities	Two spade tricks once ♠A is forced out. See Chapter 4. Two heart tricks, providing declarer lets the defence attack the suit again. Extra tricks can be made in both diamonds and clubs by finessing the queens, which the bidding shows must be held by South. See Chapter 13.
Threats	The defence will lead hearts every time they gain the lead to establish their heart suit. However, they should only gain the lead once more, with ♠A, so this threat should not amount to anything.
Plan	Win ♥10 return and lead ♣6 to ♣K, just in case the ♣Q is a singleton (see Chapter 10). Return ♣3 and play ♣A when South plays ♣Q. Cash ♣J then play ♦3 to ♦K. Cash ♣10 and take diamond finesse. Now lead ♠Q to set up spades and make eleven tricks, just losing the two major suit aces.

18

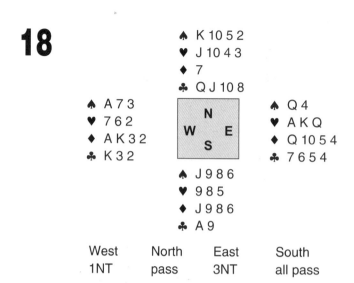

	♠ K 10 5 2	
	♥ J 10 4 3	
	♦ 7	
	♣ Q J 10 8	
♠ A 7 3		♠ Q 4
♥ 7 6 2		♥ A K Q
♦ A K 3 2		♦ Q 10 5 4
♣ K 3 2		♣ 7 6 5 4
	♠ J 9 8 6	
	♥ 9 8 5	
	♦ J 9 8 6	
	♣ A 9	

West	North	East	South
1NT	pass	3NT	all pass

North leads the ♣Q and South wins the ♣A and returns the ♣9.

Strengths	Eight top tricks after the lead sets up ♣K.
Weakness	One more trick needed.
Opportunities	It is best to hold off winning ♣K until the third round. The suit might divide 3-3, making East's ♣7 a winner. See Chapter 5. Diamonds will produce an extra trick if the suit divides 3-2 or North has a 4-card suit headed by the jack since East's Q 10 is a potential finesse position. If North has ♠K, declarer can make a trick with ♠Q if he leads small towards it before taking ♠A.
Threats	If South has four diamonds to the jack the extra diamond trick cannot be made. Keep ♦A K as entry to ♠A. See Chapter 7.
Plan	Lead a small spade towards East's ♠Q 4. If North holds ♠K, an extra trick will be established in spades and communication between the East-West hands is still available in diamonds to take it without problem. If South has ♠K, West can still look for four diamond tricks.

hands to play

19

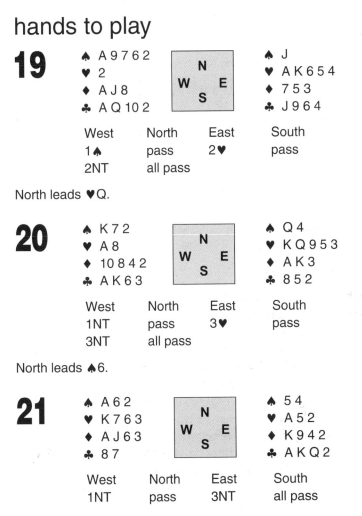

♠ A 9 7 6 2
♥ 2
♦ A J 8
♣ A Q 10 2

♠ J
♥ A K 6 5 4
♦ 7 5 3
♣ J 9 6 4

West	North	East	South
1♠	pass	2♥	pass
2NT	all pass		

North leads ♥Q.

20

♠ K 7 2
♥ A 8
♦ 10 8 4 2
♣ A K 6 3

♠ Q 4
♥ K Q 9 5 3
♦ A K 3
♣ 8 5 2

West	North	East	South
1NT	pass	3♥	pass
3NT	all pass		

North leads ♠6.

21

♠ A 6 2
♥ K 7 6 3
♦ A J 6 3
♣ 8 7

♠ 5 4
♥ A 5 2
♦ K 9 4 2
♣ A K Q 2

West	North	East	South
1NT	pass	3NT	all pass

North leads ♠Q and South follows with ♠K.

19

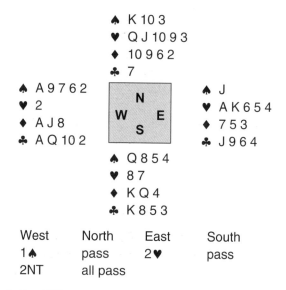

```
                ♠ K 10 3
                ♥ Q J 10 9 3
                ♦ 10 9 6 2
                ♣ 7
♠ A 9 7 6 2                        ♠ J
♥ 2              ┌─────────┐       ♥ A K 6 5 4
♦ A J 8          │    N    │       ♦ 7 5 3
♣ A Q 10 2       │  W   E  │       ♣ J 9 6 4
                 │    S    │
                 └─────────┘
                ♠ Q 8 5 4
                ♥ 8 7
                ♦ K Q 4
                ♣ K 8 5 3
```

West	North	East	South
1♠	pass	2♥	pass
2NT	all pass		

North leads the ♥Q.

Strengths	Five top tricks.
Weakness	Three more tricks needed.
Opportunities	Clubs, finessing South for ♣K.
Threats	The lead is inconvenient since it disrupts communications. Say declarer wins the initial lead in dummy to play ♣J at trick two. South does not cover and so ♣J wins that trick. West breathes a sigh of relief and realises that he has to take the second top winner in hearts, while he still has the lead with East for the last time. He then repeats the club finesse. South plays small and ♣10 wins but unfortunately the 4-1 break means that the suit can produce only three tricks. There is no further entry to dummy to finesse for the third time.
Plan	West was right to finesse in clubs, but it was a mistake to start with ♣J. Can you see the difference in leading ♣9 to take the first finesse and ♣J to repeat it? See Chapter 7.

20

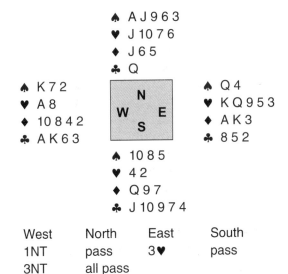

- ♠ A J 9 6 3
- ♥ J 10 7 6
- ♦ J 6 5
- ♣ Q

- ♠ K 7 2
- ♥ A 8
- ♦ 10 8 4 2
- ♣ A K 6 3

- ♠ Q 4
- ♥ K Q 9 5 3
- ♦ A K 3
- ♣ 8 5 2

- ♠ 10 8 5
- ♥ 4 2
- ♦ Q 9 7
- ♣ J 10 9 7 4

West	North	East	South
1NT	pass	3♥	pass
3NT	all pass		

North leads ♠6.

Strengths	Seven top winners.
Weakness	Two more tricks needed.
Opportunities	Spades must produce one more trick and hearts should deliver the second trick required.
Threats	Provided that West correctly plays East's ♠Q on the first trick, his ♠K 7 protects the suit from a further spade lead by North. This is a classic danger hand position: West can afford to lose the lead to North, but not to South since, should that hand get in, a spade through West will mean the loss of four spade tricks. See Chapter 15.
Plan	Lead a small heart from East at trick two. West plays ♥8 if South plays low! North is welcome to that trick while the spades are still protected. Of course, if South produces ♥J or ♥10, West would have to take ♥A. As it happens, playing off the three top hearts also works because it is North who, unexpectedly, has the length in hearts.

21

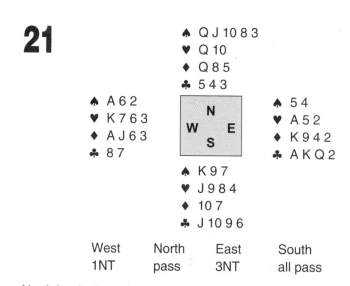

```
              ♠ Q J 10 8 3
              ♥ Q 10
              ♦ Q 8 5
              ♣ 5 4 3
♠ A 6 2          N          ♠ 5 4
♥ K 7 6 3    W       E      ♥ A 5 2
♦ A J 6 3        S          ♦ K 9 4 2
♣ 8 7                       ♣ A K Q 2
              ♠ K 9 7
              ♥ J 9 8 4
              ♦ 10 7
              ♣ J 10 9 6
```

West	North	East	South
1NT	pass	3NT	all pass

North leads the ♠Q and South plays the ♠K.

Strengths	Eight top tricks.
Weakness	One more trick needed.
Opportunities	An extra trick in diamonds must be established.
Threats	West must hold up ♠A until the third round. The point of this is to make sure South has no spade to lead back if the suit is breaking 5-3. North is the danger hand and must be kept off lead. See Chapter 15.
Plan	Normally, West would finesse ♦J in his own hand but, because North is the known danger hand, it means that a variation must be employed. To give himself the best chance, after being forced to win ♠A, declarer should cash ♦A and then lead a diamond towards East's ♦K 9 4 and finesse the nine if North follows small. He doesn't mind losing the lead to the safe (South) hand even if ♦10 takes this trick. It means that the suit has broken 3-2 and the extra trick is assured. See Chapter 16.

hands to play

22

♠ Q 7			♠ 6 4 3
♥ Q 9 3		N	♥ A 8 2
♦ A Q 4	W	E	♦ K J 10
♣ K 7 6 3 2		S	♣ A Q 9 5

West	North	East	South
1NT	pass	3NT	all pass

North leads ♥7.

23

♠ K Q			♠ 10 6
♥ A K Q		N	♥ 7 4
♦ K Q J 10 9	W	E	♦ 7 5 3
♣ 9 8 5		S	♣ A Q 7 4 3 2

West	North	East	South
2NT	pass	3NT	all pass

North leads ♠5.

24

♠ A K Q			♠ J 5 3
♥ 7 4 2		N	♥ A K Q
♦ A K 9 4 3	W	E	♦ J 5 2
♣ J 7		S	♣ A K 4 3

West	North	East	South
1♦	pass	2♣	pass
3NT	pass	6NT	all pass

North leads ♠10.

22

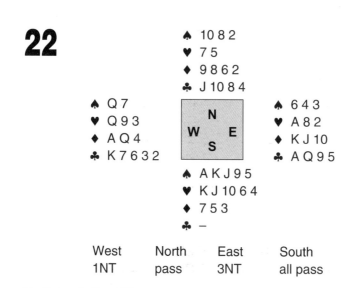

♠ 10 8 2
♥ 7 5
♦ 9 8 6 2
♣ J 10 8 4

♠ Q 7
♥ Q 9 3
♦ A Q 4
♣ K 7 6 3 2

♠ 6 4 3
♥ A 8 2
♦ K J 10
♣ A Q 9 5

♠ A K J 9 5
♥ K J 10 6 4
♦ 7 5 3
♣ —

West	North	East	South
1NT	pass	3NT	all pass

North leads the ♥7.

Strengths	Seven top tricks.
Weakness	Two more tricks needed.
Opportunities	Clubs will yield one or two tricks. ♥Q can take a trick if South has ♥K.
Threats	Spades look very vulnerable with ♠Q the highest of only five cards between the two hands. Declarer was lucky they led hearts. The lead looks like it might be fourth best. But if it isn't South will win the trick and switch to a spade, so win the opening lead. The contract is also threatened if the clubs break unkindly.
Plan	Clubs do break badly. If declarer plays ♣A or ♣Q at trick two, he is unable to make five club tricks. However, if he plays a low club towards West's ♣K, South shows out and West can lead twice towards East's ♣A Q 9 sitting over North's ♣J 10 8. Both times East's hand simply covers whatever North plays. If the clubs had been the other way round there would be nothing declarer could do.

24

♠ 10 9 8 7	
♥ J 6	
♦ Q 10 8 7	
♣ Q 10 8	

♠ A K Q		N		♠ J 5 3
♥ 7 4 2	W		E	♥ A K Q
♦ A K 9 4 3		S		♦ J 5 2
♣ J 7				♣ A K 4 3

♠ 6 4 2	
♥ 10 9 8 5 3	
♦ 6	
♣ 9 6 5 2	

West	North	East	South
1♦	pass	2♣	pass
3NT	pass	6NT	all pass

North leads the ♠ 10.

Strengths	Ten top tricks.
Weakness	Two more tricks needed.
Opportunities	The expected 3-2 break in diamonds should supply the two extra tricks required.
Threats	The diamonds may not break 3-2. A small diamond from West towards East's J 5 2 would be a reasonable line and it works here. But what if South had ♦Q singleton? (Note that we have not been that unfair!)
Plan	West can guarantee four diamond tricks, against any 4-1 break, by starting with a top diamond and then playing towards East's ♦ J 5. The bad break will come to light when the second diamond is played. If North has four diamonds, the jack becomes one trick and West's fifth diamond another. If South has four diamonds, South's queen will win, but West, with ♦ K 9 4, sits over South's ♦ 10 8 and this is a finesse position.

23

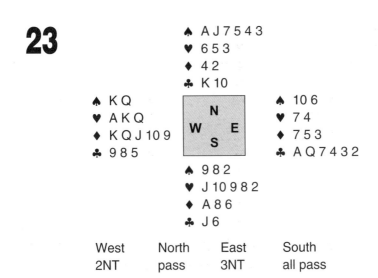

North
- ♠ A J 7 5 4 3
- ♥ 6 5 3
- ♦ 4 2
- ♣ K 10

West
- ♠ K Q
- ♥ A K Q
- ♦ K Q J 10 9
- ♣ 9 8 5

East
- ♠ 10 6
- ♥ 7 4
- ♦ 7 5 3
- ♣ A Q 7 4 3 2

South
- ♠ 9 8 2
- ♥ J 10 9 8 2
- ♦ A 8 6
- ♣ J 6

West	North	East	South
2NT	pass	3NT	all pass

North leads ♠5.

Strengths	Four top tricks and one on the lead.
Weakness	Five more tricks needed.
Opportunities	West had great expectations of his diamond suit when he opened the bidding. Clubs are the only other possibility.
Threats	The spade threat dooms the contract if declarer loses the lead. This means the diamond suit is now useless because the defenders will be able to gain the lead with ♦A if declarer leads the suit.
Plan	It's time for great courage: West must take the club finesse and pray, not only that ♣K is with North, but that the suit breaks 2-2. West must start with ♣9 to dummy's ♣Q and play ♣8 on the ♣A, keeping the ♣5 to play on East's ♣7 in order not to block the suit. Played correctly, ten tricks will be made but not a single one of them will come from diamonds, the suit that promised great things when West first looked at his hand.